Anonymous

Military Notes on Puerto Rico

Vol. 1

Anonymous

Military Notes on Puerto Rico
Vol. 1

ISBN/EAN: 9783337380434

Printed in Europe, USA, Canada, Australia, Japan

Cover: Foto ©ninafisch / pixelio.de

More available books at **www.hansebooks.com**

ADJUT
MILI

MIL   S

'UE   CO.

GO

INTRODUCTORY NOTE.

The following notes were compiled for the information of the Army, and embody all reliable information available. Many of the books consulted in the preparation are old editions, and therefore errors due to recent changes may be frequent.

The notes are intended to supplement the Military Map of Puerto Rico. The small scale index map will be of use in locating the principal cities and handy for referring to the other charts and plans attached to these notes.

By permission of the Chief Hydrographer, United States Navy, the sailing directions for Mona Passage and the island of Puerto Rico have been reprinted in full and added to these notes as a supplement.

The following books and works were consulted and matter from them freely used in the preparation of the notes:

Guía Geográfico Militar de España y Provincias Ultramarinas, 1879.

España, sus Monumentos y Artes, su Naturaleza é Historia, 1887.
Compendio de Geografía Militar de España y Portugal, 1882.
Anuario de Comercio de España, 1896.
Anuario Militar de España, 1898.
Réclus, Nouvelle Géographie Universelle, 1891.
Advance Sheets American Consular Reports, 1898.
An Account of the Present State of the Island of Puerto Rico, 1834.
The Statesman's Year Book, 1898.

WASHINGTON, *July, 1898.*

TABLE OF CONTENTS.

	Page.
Situation	7
Size	7
Population	7
Soil	7
Climate	7
Storms	10
Earthquakes	11
Tides	11
Orography	11
Approximate height of towns above sea level	12
Hydrography	12
Coasts, harbors, bays, and coves	14
Highways	16
Railroads	18
Telegraphs	19
Telephones	19
Administration	20
Education	20
Agriculture, industry, and commerce	20
Adjacent islands	20
Table of distances between principal cities	22
Cities, villages, etc	23
Stations and strength of Spanish troops	40

SUPPLEMENT.

Sailing directions for Puerto Rico and Mona Passage	49

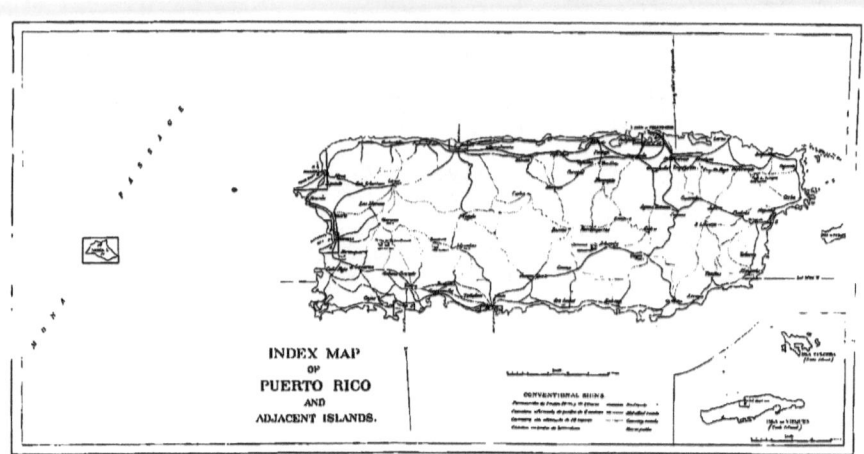

MILITARY NOTES ON PUERTO RICO.

Situation.—Puerto Rico is situated in the Torrid Zone, in the easternmost part of the Antilles, between latitude 17° 54' and 18° 30' 40" N. and longitude 61° 54' 26" and 63° 32' 32" W. of Madrid. It is bounded on the north by the Atlantic, on the east and south by the sea of the Antilles, and on the west by the Mona Channel.

Size.—The island of Puerto Rico, the fourth in size of the Antilles, has, according to a recent report of the British consul (1897), an extent of about 3,668 square miles—35 miles broad and 95 miles long. It is of an oblong form, extending from east to west.

Population.—Puerto Rico is the first among the Antilles in density of population and in prosperity. The Statesman's Year Book, 1898, gives the population (1887) at 813,937, of which over 300,000 are negroes, this being one of the few countries of tropical America where the number of whites exceeds that of other races. The whites and colored, however, are all striving in the same movement of civilization, and are gradually becoming more alike in ideas and manners. Among the white population the number of males exceeds the number of females, which is the contrary of all European countries. This is partly explained by the fact that the immigrants are mostly males. On an average the births exceed the deaths by double. The eastern portion of the island is less populous than the western.

Soil.—The ground is very fertile, being suitable for the cultivation of cane, coffee, rice, and other products raised in Cuba, which island Puerto Rico resembles in richness and fertility.

Climate.—The climate is hot and moist, the medium temperature reaching 104° F. Constant rains and winds from the east cool the heavy atmosphere of the low regions. On the heights of the Central Cordillera the temperature is healthy and agreeable.

Iron rusts and becomes consumed, so that nothing can be constructed of this metal. Even bronze artillery has to be covered with a strong varnish to protect it from the damp winds.

Although one would suppose that all the large islands in the Tropics enjoyed the same climate, yet from the greater mortality observed in Jamaica, St. Domingo, and Cuba, as compared with Puerto Rico, one is inclined to believe that this latter island is much more congenial than any of the former to the health of

Europeans. The heat, the rains, and the seasons are, with very trifling variations, the same in all. But the number of mountains and running streams, which are everywhere in view in Puerto Rico, and the general cultivation of the land, may powerfully contribute to purify the atmosphere and render it salubrious to man. The only difference of temperature to be observed throughout the island is due to altitude, a change which is common to every country under the influence of the Tropics.

In the mountains the inhabitants enjoy the coolness of spring, while the valleys would be uninhabitable were it not for the daily breeze which blows generally from the northeast and east. For example, in Ponce the noonday sun is felt in all its rigor, while at the village of Adjuntas, 4 leagues distant in the interior of the mountains, the traveler feels invigorated by the refreshing breezes of a temperate clime. At one place the thermometer is as high as 90°, while in another it is sometimes under 60°. Although the seasons are not so distinctly marked in this climate as they are in Europe (the trees being always green), yet there is a distinction to be made between them. The division into wet and dry seasons (winter and summer) does not give a proper idea of the seasons in this island; for on the north coast it sometimes rains almost the whole year, while sometimes for twelve or fourteen months not a drop of rain falls on the south coast. However, in the mountains at the south there are daily showers. Last year, for example, in the months of November, December, and January the north winds blew with violence, accompanied by heavy showers of rain, while this year (1832) in the same months, it has scarcely blown a whole day from that point of the compass, nor has it rained for a whole month. Therefore, the climate of the north and south coasts of this island, although under the same tropical influence, are essentially different.

As in all tropical countries, the year is divided into two seasons—the dry and the rainy. In general, the rainy season commences in August and ends the last of December, southerly and westerly winds prevailing during this period. The rainfall is excessive, often inundating fields and forming extensive lagoons. The exhalations from these lagoons give rise to a number of diseases, but, nevertheless, Puerto Rico is one of the healthiest islands of the Archipelago.

In the month of May the rains commence, not with the fury of a deluge, as in the months of August and September, but heavier than any rain experienced in Europe. Peals of thunder reverberating through the mountains give a warning of their approach, and the sun breaking through the clouds promotes the prolific vegetation of the fields with its vivifying heat. The heat at this season is equal to the summer of Europe, and the nights are cool and pleasant; but the dews are heavy and pernicious to health. The following meteorological observations, carefully made by Don José Ma. Vertéz, a captain of the Spanish navy, will exhibit the average range of the temperature:

Degrees of heat observed in the capital of Puerto Rico, taking a medium of five years.

Hours of the day.	Jan.	Feb.	Mar.	Apr.	May.	June.	July.	Aug.	Sept.	Oct.	Nov.	Dec.
Seven in the morning	72	72½	74	78	78	82	85	86	80½	77	75	75
Noon	82	81	82	83	85	86	90	92	88	85	84	80
Five in the evening	78	74	78	80	81	84	87	90	83	82	80	79

The weather, after a fifteen or twenty days' rain, clears up, and the sun, whose heat has been hitherto moderated by partial clouds and showers of rain, seems, as it were, set in a cloudless sky. The cattle in the pastures look for the shade of the trees, and a perfect calm pervades the whole face of nature from sunrise till between 10 and 11 o'clock in the morning, when the sea breeze sets in. The leaves of the trees seem as if afraid to move, and the sea, without a wave or a ruffle on its vast expanse, appears like an immense mirror. Man partakes in the general languor as well as the vegetable and brute creation.

The nights, although warm, are delightfully clear and serene at this season. Objects may be clearly distinguished at the distance of several hundred yards, so that one may even shoot by moonlight. The months of June and July offer very little variation in the weather or temperature. In August a suffocating heat reigns throughout the day, and at night it is useless to seek for coolness; a faint zephyr is succeeded by a calm of several hours. The atmosphere is heavy and oppressive, and the body, weakened by perspiration, becomes languid; the appetite fails, and the mosquitoes, buzzing about the ears by day and night, perplex and annoy by their stings, while the fevers of the tropics attack Europeans with sudden and irresistible violence. This is the most sickly season for the European. The thermometer frequently exceeds 90°. The clouds exhibit a menacing appearance, portending the approach of the heavy autumnal rains, which pour down like a deluge. About the middle of September it appears as if all the vapors of the ocean had accumulated in one point of the heavens. The rain comes down like an immense quantity of water poured through a sieve; it excludes from the view every surrounding object, and in half an hour the whole surface of the earth becomes an immense sheet of water. The rivers are swollen and overflow their banks, the low lands are completely inundated, and the smallest brooks become deep and rapid torrents.

In the month of October the weather becomes sensibly cooler than during the preceding months, and in November the north and northeast, winds generally set in, diffusing an agreeable coolness through the surrounding atmosphere. The body becomes braced and active, and the convalescent feels its genial influence.

The north wind is accompanied (with few exceptions) by heavy showers of rain on the north coast; and the sea rolls on that coast with tempestuous violence, while the south coast remains perfectly calm.

When the fury of the north wind abates, it is succeeded by fine weather and a clear sky. Nothing can exceed the climate of Puerto Rico at this season; one can only compare it to the month of May in the delightful Province of Andalusia, where the cold of winter and the burning heat of summer are tempered by the cool freshness of spring. This is considered to be the healthiest season of the year, when a European may visit the tropics without fear.

The small islands, destitute of wood and high mountains, which have a powerful effect in attracting the clouds, suffer much from drought. It sometimes happens that in Curaçao, St. Bartholomews, and other islands there are whole years without a drop of rain, and after exhausting their cisterns the inhabitants are compelled to import water from the rivers of other islands.

"The land breeze" is an advantage which the large islands derive from the inequality of their surface; for as soon as the sea breeze dies away, the hot air of the valleys being rarefied, ascends toward the tops of the mountains, and is there condensed by cold, which makes it specifically heavier than it was before; it then descends back to the valleys on both sides of the ridge. Hence a night wind (blowing on all sides from the land toward the shore) is felt in all the mountainous countries under the torrid zone. On the north shore the wind comes from the south, and on the south shore from the north.

Storms.—The hurricanes which visit the island, and which obey the general laws of tropical cyclones, are one of the worst scourges of the country. For hours before the appearance of this terrible phenomenon the sea appears calm; the waves come from a long distance very gently until near the shore, when they suddenly rise as if impelled by a superior force, dashing against the land with extraordinary violence and fearful noise. Together with this sign, the air is noticed to be disturbed, the sun red, and the stars obscured by a vapor which seems to magnify them. A strong odor is perceived in the sea, which is sulphureous in the waters of rivers, and there are sudden changes in the wind. These omens, together with the signs of uneasiness manifested by various animals, foretell the proximity of a hurricane.

This is a sort of whirlwind, accompanied by rain, thunder, and lightning, sometimes by earthquake shocks, and always by the most terrible and devastating circumstances that can possibly combine to ruin a country in a few hours. A clear, serene day is followed by the darkest night; the delightful view offered by woods and prairies is diverted into the dreary waste of a cruel winter; the tallest and most robust cedar trees are uprooted, broken off bodily, and hurled into a heap; roofs, balconies, and windows of houses are carried through the air like dry leaves, and in all directions are seen houses and estates laid waste and thrown into confusion.

The fierce roar of the water and of the trees being destroyed by the winds, the cries and moans of persons, the bellowing of cattle and neighing of horses, which are being carried from place to place by the whirlwinds, the torrents of water inundating the fields, and a deluge of fire being let loose in flashes and streaks of lightning, seem to announce the last convulsions of the universe and the death agonies of nature itself.

Sometimes these hurricanes are felt only on the north coast, at others on the south coast, although generally their influence extends throughout the island.

In 1825 a hurricane destroyed the towns of Patillas, Maunabo, Yabucoa, Humacao, Gurabo, and Caguas, causing much damage in other towns in the east, north, and center of the island. The island was also visited by a terrible hurricane in 1772.

Earthquakes.—Earthquakes are somewhat frequent, but not violent or of great consequence. The natives foretell them by noticing clouds settle near the ground for some time in the open places among the mountains. The water of the springs emits a sulphurous odor or leaves a strange taste in the mouth; birds gather in large flocks and fly about uttering shriller cries than usual; cattle bellow and horses neigh, etc. A few hours beforehand the air becomes calm and dimmed by vapors which arise from the ground, and a few moments before there is a slight breeze, followed at intervals of two or three minutes by a deep rumbling noise, accompanied by a sudden gust of wind, which are the forerunners of the vibration, the latter following immediately. These shocks are sometimes violent and are usually repeated, but owing to the special construction of the houses, they cause no damage.

Tides.—For seven hours the tide runs rapidly in a northwest direction, returning in the opposite direction with equal rapidity for five hours.

Orography.—The general relief of Puerto Rico is much inferior in altitude to that of the rest of the Great Antilles, and even some of the Lesser Antilles have mountain summits which rival it.

A great chain of mountains divides the islands into two parts, northern and southern, which are called by the natives Banda del Norte and Banda del Sur. This chain sends out long ramifications toward the coasts, the interstices of which form beautiful and fertile valleys, composed in the high parts of white and red earths, on the spurs of black and weaker earths, and near the coasts of sand.

To the northwest and following a direction almost parallel with the northern coast, the Sierra of Lares extends from Aguadilla to the town of Lares, where it divides into two branches, one going north nearly to the coast, near Arecibo Harbor, and the other extending to the spurs of the Sierra Grande de Baños; this latter starting from Point Guaniquilla, crosses the island in its entire length, its last third forming the Sierra of Cayey.

The whole island may be said to form a continuous network of sierras, hills, and heights. Of these the Sierra del Loquillo is distinguished for its great altitude (the highest peak being Yunque, in the northeast corner of the island and visible from the sea, a distance of 120 kilometers), as is also Laivonito Mountain, near the south coast.

The following are the four highest mountains, with their heights above the sea level: Yunque, in Luquillo, 1,290 yards; Guilarte, in Adjuntas, 1,180 yards; La Somanta, in Aybonito, 1,077 yards; Las Tetas de Cerro Gordo, in San German, 860 yards. All are easily ascended on foot or horseback, and there are coffee plantations near all of them.

Approximate height of towns above the sea level.—Aybonito, with its acclimatization station, 970 yards; Adjuntas, an almost exclusively Spanish town, 810 yards; Cayey, with a very agreeable climate, 750 yards; Lares, with a very agreeable climate, 540 yards; Utuado, with a very agreeable climate, 480 yards; Muricao, an exclusively Spanish town, 480 yards. To ascend to all these towns there are very good wagon roads. There are no fortifications of any kind in them, but they are surrounded on all sides by mountains.

Hydrography.—Few countries of the extent of Puerto Rico are watered by so many streams. Seventeen rivers, taking their rise in the mountains, cross the valleys of the north coast and empty into the sea. Some of these are navigable 2 or 3 leagues from their mouths for schooners and small coasting vessels. Those of Manatí, Loisa, Trabajo, and Arecibo are very deep and broad, and it is difficult to imagine how such large bodies of water can be collected in so short a course. Owing to the heavy surf which continually breaks on the north coast, these rivers have bars across their embouchures which do not allow large vessels to enter. The rivers of Bayamo and Rio Piedras flow into the harbor of the capital, and are also navigable for boats. At high water small brigs may enter the river of Arecibo with perfect safety and discharge their cargoes, notwithstanding the bar which crosses its mouth.

The rivers of the north coast have a decided advantage over those of the south coast, where the climate is drier and the rains less frequent. Nevertheless, the south, west, and east coasts are well supplied with water; and, although in some seasons it does not rain for ten, and sometimes twelve months on the south coast, the rivers are never entirely dried up.

From the Cabeza de San Juan, which is the northeast extremity of the island, to the cape of Mala Pascua, which lies to the southeast, 9 rivers fall into the sea.

From Cape Mala Pascua to Point Aguila, which forms the southwest angle of the island, 16 rivers discharge their waters on the south coast.

On the west coast 3 rivers, 5 rivulets, and several fresh-water lakes communicate with the sea. In the small extent of 330 leagues of area there are 46 rivers, besides a countless number of rivulets and branches of navigable water.

The rivers of the north coast are stocked with delicious fish, some of them large enough to weigh two quintals.

From the river of Arecibo to that of Manatí, a distance of 5 leagues, a fresh-water lagoon, perfectly navigable for small vessels through the whole of its extent, runs parallel to the sea at about a mile from the shore.

In the fertile valley of Añasco, on the western coast, there is a canal formed by nature, deep and navigable. None of the rivers are of real military importance; for, though considering the shortness of their course, they attain quite a volume, still it is not sufficient for good-sized vessels.

The rivers emptying on the north coast are Loisa, Aguas Prietas, Arecibo, Bayamón, Camuy, Cedros, Grande, Guajataca de la Tuna, Lesayas, Loquillo, Manatí, Rio Piedras, Sabana, San Martín, Sibuco, Toa, and Vega.

Those emptying on the east coast are Candelero, Dagua, Fajardo, Guayanes, Majogua, and Maonabo.

On the south coast: Aquamanil, Caballon, Caña, Coamo, Descalabrado, Guanica, Guayama, Guayanilla, Jacagua, Manglar, Peñuela, Ponce, and Vigia.

On the west coast: Aguada, Boquerón, Cajas, Culebrina, Chico, Guanajibo, Mayagüez, and Rincon.

The limits of the Loisa River are: On the east, the sierra of Luquillo (situated near the northeast corner of the island); on the south, the sierra of Cayey, and on the west, ramifications of the latter. It rises in the northern slopes of the sierra of Cayey, and, running in a northwest direction for the first half of its course and turning to northeast in the second half, it arrives at Loisa, a port on the northern coast, where it discharges its waters into the Atlantic. During the first part of its course it is known by the name of Cayagua.

The Sabana River has, to the east and south, the western and southern limits of the preceding river, and on the west the Sierra Grande, or De Barros, which is situated in the center of the general divide or watershed. It rises in the sierra of Cayey, and, with the name of Piñones River, it flows northwest, passing through Aibonito, Toa Alta, Toa Baja, and Dorado, where it discharges into the Atlantic to the west of the preceding river.

The Manatí River is bounded on the east and south by the Sierra Grande and on the west by the Siales ridge. It rises in the Sierra Grande, and parallel with the preceding river, it flows through Siales and Manatí, to the north of which latter town it empties into the Atlantic.

The Arecibo River is bounded on the east by the Siales Mountain ridge, on the south by the western extremity of the Sierra Grande, and on the west by the Lares ridge. It rises in the general divide, near Adjuntas, and flows north through the town of Arecibo to the Atlantic, shortly before emptying into which it receives the Tanama River from the left, which proceeds from the Lares Mountains.

The Culebrina River is bounded on the south and east by the Lares Mountain ridge, and on the north by small hills of little interest. From the Lares Mountains it flows from east to west and empties on the west coast north of San Francisco de la Aguada, in the center of the bay formed between Point Peñas Blancas and Point San Francisco.

The Añasco River is formed by the Lares Mountain ridge. It rises in the eastern extremity of the mountains called Tetas de Cerro Gordo, flowing first northwest, and then west, through the town of its name and thence to the sea.

The Guanajivo River has to its north the ramification of the Lares ridge, to the east the Tetas de Cerro Gordo Mountains, and on the south Torre Hill. In the interior of its basin is the mountain called Cerro Montuoso, which separates its waters from those of its affluent from the right, the Rosario River. It rises in the general divide, flowing from east to west to Nuestra Señora de Montserrat, where it receives the affluent mentioned, the two together then emptying south of Port Mayagüez.

The Coamo River is bounded on the west and north by the Sierra Grande, and on the east by the Coamo ridge. It rises in the former of these sierras, and flowing from north to south it empties east of Coamo Point, after having watered the town of its name.

The Salinas River is bounded on the west by the Coamo ridge, on the north by the general divide, and on the east by the Cayey ridge. It rises in the southern slopes of the Sierra Grande and flowing from north to south through Salinas de Coamo, empties into the sea.

Coasts, harbors, bays, and coves.—The northern coasts extends in an almost straight line from east to west, and is high and rugged. The only harbors it has are the following: San Juan de Puerto Rico, surrounded by mangrove swamps and protected by the Cabras and the Cabritas islands and some very dangerous banks; the anchoring ground of Arecibo, somewhat unprotected; and the coves of Caugrejos and Condado. During the months of November, December, and January, when the wind blows with violence from the east and northeast, the anchorage is dangerous in all the bays and harbors of this coast, except in the port of San Juan. Vessels are often obliged to put to sea on the menacing aspect of the heavens at this season, to avoid being driven on shore by the heavy squalls and the rolling waves of a boisterous sea, which propel them to destruction. During the remaining months the ports on this coast are safe and commodious, unless when visited by a hurricane, against whose fury no port can offer a shelter, nor any vessel be secure. The excellent port of San Juan is perfectly sheltered from the effects of the north wind. The hill, upon which the town of that name and the fortifications which defend it are built, protects the vessels anchored in the harbor. The entrance of this port is narrow, and requires a pilot; for the canal which leads to the anchorage, although deep enough for vessels of any dimensions, is very narrow, which exposes them to run aground. This port is several miles in extent, and has the advantage of having deep canals to the east, among a wood of mangrove trees, where vessels are perfectly secure during the hurricane months. Vessels of 250 tons can at present unload and take in their cargoes at the wharf. Harbor improvements have been recently made here.

On the northwest and west are the coves of Aguadilla, the town of this name being some 4 kilometers inland. There are the small coves of Rincón, Añasco, and Mayagüez, the latter being protected and of sufficient depth to anchor vessels of moderate draft; the harbor of Real de Cabo Rojo, nearly round, and entered by a narrow channel; and the cove of Boquerón. The spacious bay of Aguadilla is formed by Cape Borrigna and Cape San Francisco. When the north-northwest and southwest winds prevail it is not a safe anchorage for ships. A heavy surf rolling on the shore obliges vessels to seek safety by putting to sea on the appearance of a north wind. Mayagüez is also an open roadstead formed by two projecting capes. It has good anchorage for vessels of a large size and is well sheltered from the north winds. The port of Cabo Rojo has also good anchorage. It is situated S. ¼ N. of the point of Guanajico, at a distance of 5½ miles. Its shape is nearly circular, and it extends from east to west 3 to 4 miles. At the entrance it has 3 fathoms of water, and 16 feet in the middle of the harbor. The entrance is a narrow canal.

The south coast abounds in bays and harbors, but is covered with mangroves and reefs, the only harbor where vessels of regular draft can enter being Guanica and Ponce. The former of these is the westernmost harbor on the southern coast, being at the same time the best, though the least visited, owing to the swamps and low tracts difficult to cross leading from it to the interior. The nearest towns, San Germán, Sabana Grande, and Yauco, carry on a small trade through this port.

In the port of Guanica, vessels drawing 21 feet of water may enter with perfect safety. Its entrance is about 100 yards wide, and it forms a spacious basin, completely landlocked. The vessels may anchor close to the shore. It has, in the whole extent, from 6½ to 3 fathoms, the latter depth being formed in the exterior of the port. The entrance is commanded by two small hills on either side, which if mounted with a few pieces of artillery would defy a squadron to force it. This port would be of immense advantage in time of war. The national vessels and coasters would thus have a secure retreat from an enemy's cruiser on the south coast. There are no wharves, but vessels could disembark troops by running alongside the land and running out a plank. Coamo Cove and Aguirre and Guayama are also harbors. The port of Jovos, near Guayama, is a haven of considerable importance. It is a large and healthy place, and the most Spanish of any city on the island after San Juan. There are good roads to the capital. Vessels of the largest kind may anchor and ride in safety from the winds, and the whole British navy would find room in its spacious bosom. It has 4 fathoms of water in the shallowest part of the entrance. However, it is difficult to enter this port from June to November, as the sea breaks with violence at the entrance. on account of the southerly winds which reign at that season. It has every convenience of situation and locality for forming docks for the repair of shipping. The large bay of Añasco, on the south coast, affords anchorage to vessels of all sizes. It is also safe from the north winds. Although on the eastern coast there are many places for vessels to anchor, yet none of them are exempt from danger during the north winds except Fajardo, where a safe anchorage is to be found to leeward of two little islands close to the bay, where vessels are completely sheltered.

The island of Vieques has also several commodious ports and harbors, where vessels of the largest size may ride at anchor.

On the east coast is Cape Cabeza de San Juan, Points Lima, Candeleros, and Naranjo, and Cape Mala Pascua; on the south coast, Point Viento, Tigueras, Corchones, Arenas, Fama or Maria, Cucharas, Guayanilla, Guanica, and Morrillos de Cabo Rojo; on the west coast, points San Francisco, Cadena, Guanijito, Guaniquilla, and Palo Seco.

Highways.—There are few roads or ways of communication which are worthy of mention, with the exception of the broad pike which starts from the capital and runs along the coast, passing through the following towns: Aguadilla, Bayamón, Cabo Rojo, Humacao, Juana Díaz, Mayagüez, Ponce, and San Germán. It has no bridges; is good in dry weather, but in the rainy season is impassible for wagons and even at times for horsemen.

For interior communication there are only a few local roads or paths. They are usually 2 yards in width, made by the various owners, and can not be well traveled in rainy weather. They are more properly horse and mule trails, and oblige people to go in single file. In late years much has been attempted to improve the highways connecting the principal cities, and more has been accomplished than in Spanish colonies. There is a good made road connecting Ponce on the southern coast with San Juan, the capital. Other good roads also extend for a short distance along the north coast and along the south coast. The road from Guayama is also said to be a passably good one.

There are in the island about 150 miles of excellent road, and this is all that receives any attention, transportation being effected elsewhere on horseback. In the construction of a road level foundation is sought, and on this is put a heavy layer of crushed rock and brick, which, after having been well packed and rounded, is covered with a layer of earth. This is well packed also, and upon the whole is spread a layer of ground limestone, which is pressed and rolled until it forms almost a glossy surface. This makes an excellent road here where the climate is such that it does not affect it, and when there is no heavy traffic, but these conditions being changed, the road, it is thought, would not stand so well.

From Palo Seco, situated about a mile and a half from the capital, on the opposite side of the bay, a carriage road, perfectly level, has been constructed for a distance of 22 leagues, to the town of Aguadilla on the west coast, passing through the towns of Vegabaja, Manati, Arecibo, Hatillo, Camuy, and Isabella. This road has been carried for several leagues over swampy lands, which are intersected by deep drains to carry off the water.

The road from Aguadilla to Mayagüez is in some parts very good, in other parts only fair. From Aguadilla to Aguada, a distance of a league, the road is excellent and level. From thence to Mayagüez, through the village of Rincón and the town of Añasco, the road is generally good, but on the seashore it is sometimes interrupted by shelving rocks. Across the valley of Añasco the road is carried through a boggy tract, with bridges over several deep creeks of fresh water. From thence to the large commercial town of Mayagüez the road is uneven and requires some improvement. But the roads from Mayagüez and Ponce to their respective ports on the seashore can not be surpassed by any in Europe. They are made in a most substantial manner, and their convex form is well adapted to preserve them from the destruction caused by the heavy rains of the climate. These roads have been made over tracts of swampy ground to the seacoast, but with little and timely repair they will last forever.

A road, which may be called a carriage road, has been made from Ponce to the village of Adjuntas, situated 5 leagues in the interior of the mountains. The road along the coast, from Ponce to Guayama, is fairly good; from thence to Patillas there is an excellent carriage road for a distance of 3 leagues; from the latter place to the coast is a highroad well constructed. From Patillas to Fajardo, on the eastern coast, passing through the towns of Maimavo, Yubacao, Humacao, and Naguabo, the roads are not calculated for wheel vehicles, in consequence of being obliged to ascend and descend several steep hills. That which crosses the mountain of Mala Pascua, dividing the north and east coasts, is a good and solid road, upon which a person on horseback may travel with great ease and safety. The road crossing the valley of Yubacao, which consists of a soft and humid soil, requires more attention than that crossing the mountain of Mala Pascua, which has a fine, sandy soil.

From Fajardo to the capital, through the towns of Luquillo, Loisa, and Rio Piedras, the road is tolerably good for persons on horseback as far as Rio Piedras, and from thence to the city of San Juan, a distance of 2 leagues, is an excellent carriage road, made by the order and under the inspection of the captain-general, part of it through a mangrove swamp. Over the river Loisa is a handsome wooden bridge, and on the road near Rio Piedras is a handsome stone one over a deep rivulet.

One of the best roads in the island extends from the town of Papino, situated in the mountains, to the town of Aguadilla on the coast, distant $5\frac{1}{2}$ leagues, through the village of La Moca; in the distance of 3 leagues from the latter place. It is crossed by 10 deep mountain rivulets, formerly impassable, but over which solid bridges have now been built, with side railings. In the mountainous district within the circumference of a few leagues no less than 47 bridges have been built to facilitate the communication between one place and the other.

The following are the roads of 6 meters width, 4½ in center of pounded stone. They have iron bridges and are in good shape for travel all the year:

(1) *San Juan to the shore near Ponce.*—From San Juan to Ponce the central road is exactly 134 kilometers. Distances along the line are: Rio Piedras, 11; Caguas, 25; to Cayei, 24; Aybonito, 20; Coamo, 18; Juana Díaz, 20; to Ponce, 13; and to the shore, 3. Exact.

(2) *San Juan to Bayamon.*—By ferry fifteen minutes to Cataño, and from there by road to Bayamon 10 kilometers. This passes alongside the railway.

(3) Rio Piedras to Mameyes, 36 kilometers; from Rio Piedras to Carolina, 12; to Rio Grande, 19; to Mameyes, 5.

(4) Cayei to Arroyo, 35 kilometers; from Cayei to Guayama, 25; to Arroyo, 8; from San Juan to Arroyo, via Cayei, is 95 kilometers.

(5) Ponce to Adjuntas, 32 kilometers.

(6) San German to Añasco, 33 kilometers; from San German to Mayagüez, 21 kilometers; Mayagüez to Añasco, 12; Mayagüez to Hormigueros, 11; Mayagüez to Cabo Rojo, 18; Mayagüez to Las Marias, 23; Mayagüez to Maricao, 35; Hormigueras to San German, 14. Near Mayagüez the roads are best. There are good roads in all directions.

(7) Aguadilla to San Sebastian, 18.

(8) Arecibo to Utuado, 33.

Highways of first class in the island. 335 kilometers.

Along these roads are, at a distance of 8 to 10 kilometers, a fort, stone and brick barracks, or large buildings, where the Spanish troops stop and rest when on the march.

Railroads.—In 1878 a report was presented to the minister of the colonies on a study made by the engineer and head of public works of the island in view of constructing a railroad which should start from the capital and, passing through all the chief towns and through the whole island, return to the point of departure.

The following paragraph relating to the subject is taken from the Revista Geográfica y Estadística:

"In Puerto Rico the whistle of the locomotive is unknown, nor is there even a tramway. Enterprises of this nature are not easy of success, owing to a lack of sufficient highways to facilitate their exploitation. To show this it will suffice to recall the fact that the two principal towns of the island, Mayagüez and Ponce, do not communicate by an easy land road with the capital. Transportation is effected almost entirely by sea, and for the purpose there is but one harbor, that of the capital, it being necessary in other points of the island to await the tide in order to disembark."

Something, however, has been accomplished toward the completion of this railroad which is to encircle the entire island. The chief purpose of building this road was to facilitate the movement of Spanish troops to any part of the island.

Of this railroad the following parts have been completed: San Juan, along the coast through Rio Piedras, Bayamon, Dorado, Arecibo, and Hatillo, to Camuy; Aguadilla, through Aguado, Rincón, Añasco, and Mayagüez, to Hormigueros. A branch of this railroad from Añasco, through San Sebastian, to Lares. Ponce, through Guayanilla, to Yauco. This latter railroad follows the southern coast line and is followed by a wagon road throughout its course. In one place the railroad and road run within a few hundred yards of the coast line. According to the Statesman's Year-Book for 1898 there are in operation 137 miles of railroad, besides over 170 miles under construction.

All the railroads are single track, and the gauge is 1 meter 20 centimeters, or 3 feet 11¼ inches (47.24).

The following are the railways of 1-meter gauge:

(1) San Juan to Rio Piedras, 11 kilometers.
(2) Cataño to Bayamon, 10 kilometers.
(3) Añasco to San Sebastian and Lares, 35 kilometers.
Total of three lines, 56 kilometers.

COMPAÑIA FRANCESA, 1 METER AND 20 CENTIMETERS GAUGE.

1. San Juan to Rio Piedras, 11 kilometers, and to Carolina, 12 kilometers.
2. San Juan to Bayamon, 14; to Toa Baja, 15; to Dorado, 4; Vega Baja, 18; Manati, 12; Barceloneta, 17; to Arecíba, 8; to Hatillo, 10; to Camuey, 2. Total, 100 kilometers.
3. Line from Aguadillo to Hormiguero, 58 kilometers. Aguadillo to Aguada, 6; Rincón, 8; Añasco, 16; Mayagüez, 15; to Hormiguero, 13 kilometers.

Line from Yauco to Ponce, 35 kilometers. Yauco to Guayanillo, 12; to Tallaboa, 8; to Ponce, 15.

The lines are all in good shape; have plenty of engines and cars; speed, 20 kilometers per hour; use coal for fuel imported from the United States; supply usually large, may be small now; hard coal; fine stations; plenty of water, and everything in shape for business.

Telegraphs.—The capital communicates with the principal towns of the coast and interior by means of a well-connected telegraph system. There are in all some 470 miles of telegraph.

Telephones.—The British Consular Report says that the telephone system of San Juan, Ponce, and Mayagüez have recently been contracted for by local syndicates. In Ponce a United States company obtained the contract for the material. There are 100 stations already connected, and it is expected that 200 more will be in operation shortly.

Administration.—From an administrative standpoint, Puerto Rico is not considered as a colony, but as a province of Spain, assimilated to the remaining provinces. The governor-general, representing the monarchy, is at the same time captain-general of the armed forces. In each chief town resides a military commander, and each town has its alcalde, or mayor, appointed by the central power. The provincial deputation is elected by popular suffrage under the same conditions as in Spain. The regular peace garrison is composed of about 3,000 men, and the annual budget amounts to some 20,000,000 pesos.

Education.—In 1887 only one-seventh of the population could read and write, but of late years progress in public instruction has been rapid.

Agriculture, industry, and commerce.—In 1878 there arrived in the harbors of the island 1,591 vessels of different nationalities and 1,534 departed. The value of products imported was 14,787,551 pesos, and that of articles exported was 13,070,020 pesos. The following are the relative percentages of values:

Flags.	Relation.
	Per cent.
Spanish	49.91
American	13.47
English	21.43
Various nations	15.19
Total	100.00

Navigation is very active, but the part the inhabitants take in the commercial fleet is small. The Puerto Ricans are not seagoing people. The eastern part of the island offers less advantage to commerce than the western, being to the windward and affording less shelter to vessels.

Adjacent islands.—Adjacent to Puerto Rico on the east are the islands of Culebra, Vieques, Santa Cruz, and the group called the Virgin Islands, belonging to England and Denmark; on the west are those of Saona and Mona. The most important of these is Vieques, situated 13 miles east of Puerto Rico. It is 21 miles long and 6 miles wide, and is divided for its entire length by a chain of mountains. Its land is very fertile and adapted to the cultivation of almost all the fruits and vegetables that grow in the West Indies. Cattle are raised and sugar cultivated. The mountains are covered with timber forests. It has a population of some 6,000. The town, Isabel Segunda, is on the north, and the port is unsafe in times of northerly winds, like all the anchorages on that side. The few ports on the south are better, the best being Punta Arenas. Not long ago there were two importing and exporting houses on the island of Vieques; but, on account of the long

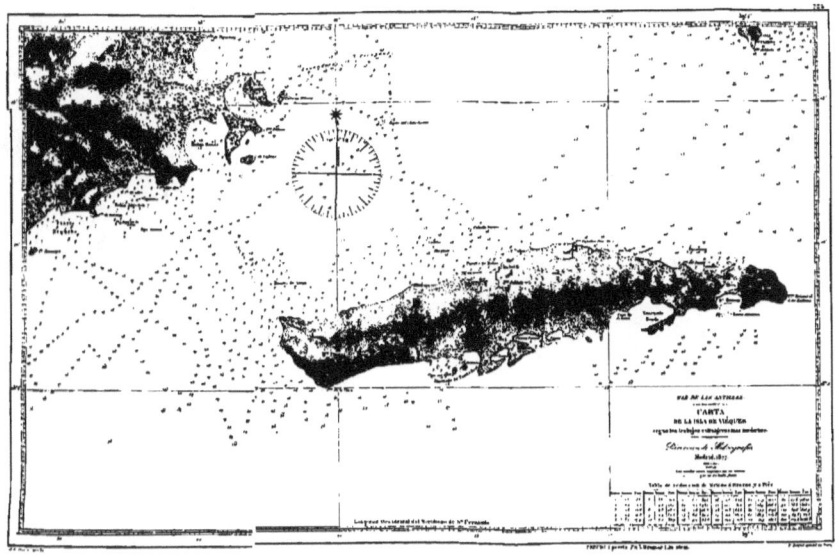

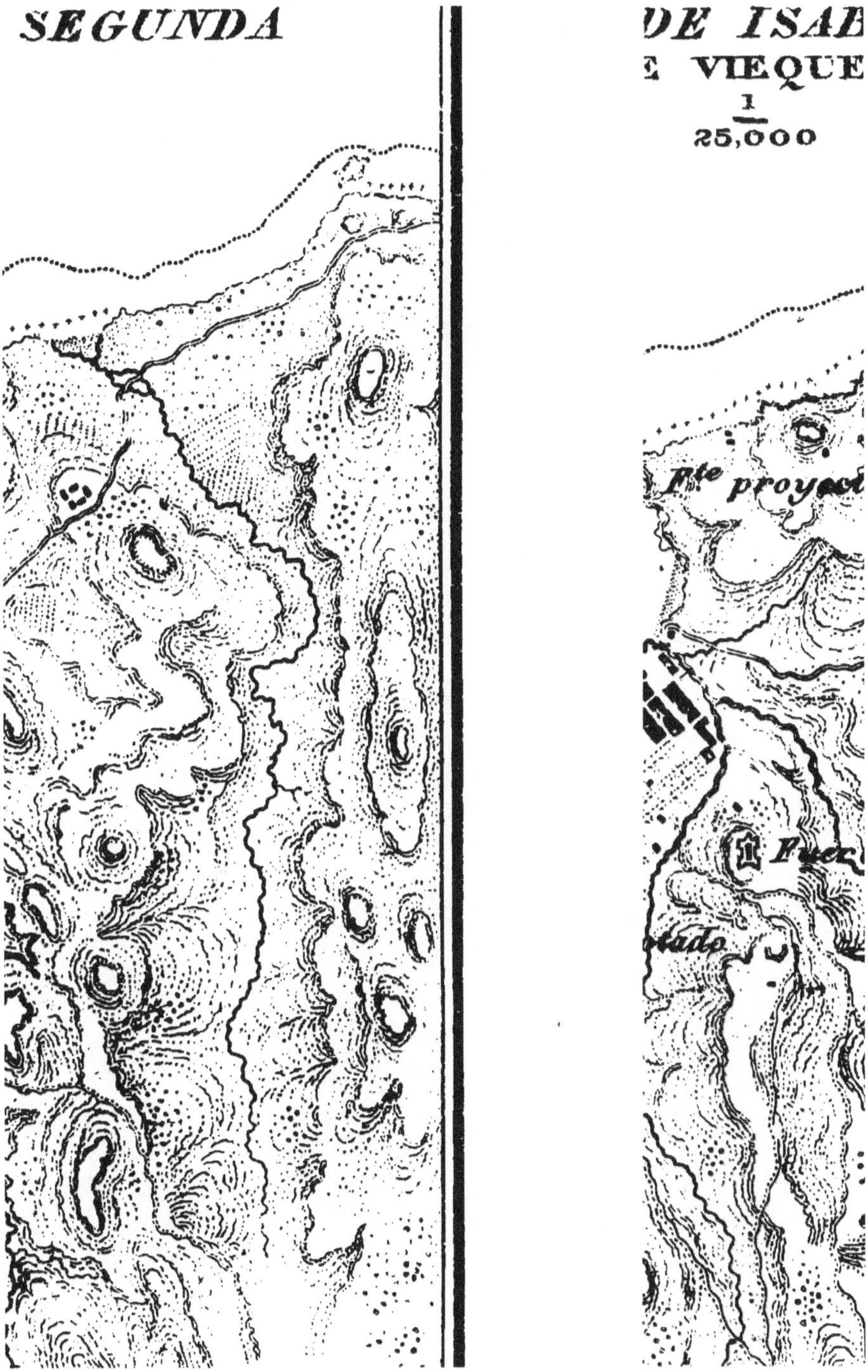

SEGUNDA DE ISABEL VIEQUE
1/25,000

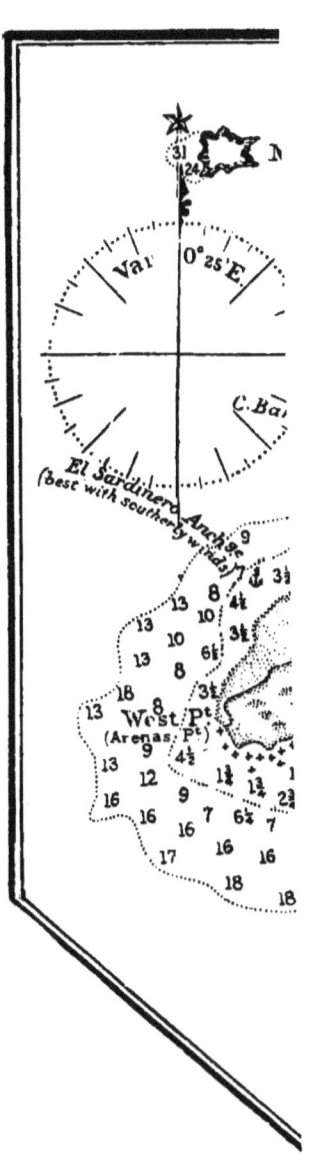

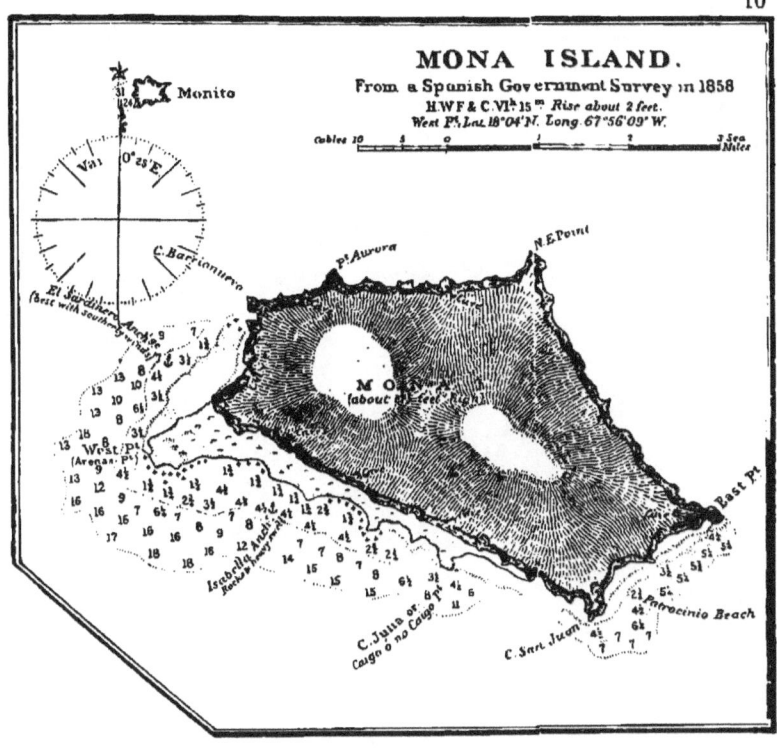

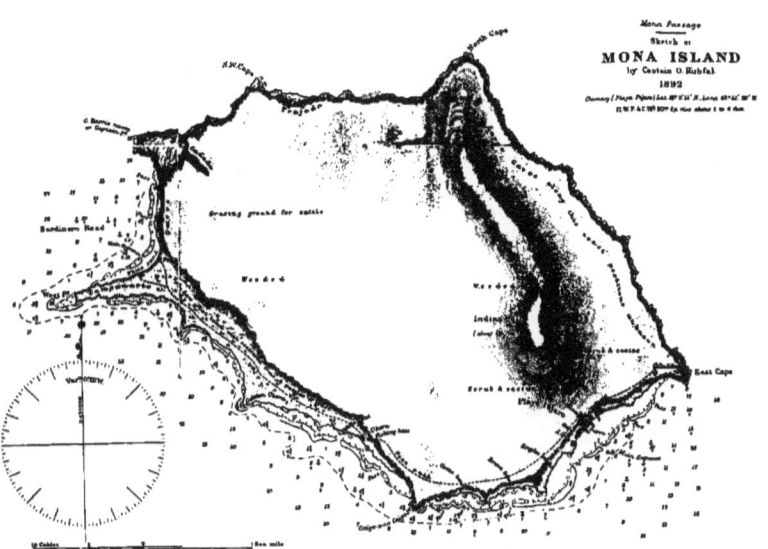

period of drought and the high duties of foreign imported goods, trade has decreased to local consumption only. All supplies are brought from San Juan, the majority being of American origin. The climate is fine and may be considered healthy; there have never been any contagious diseases.

Vieques was temporarily occupied during the two centuries preceding the present by the English and French, but is now entirely under Spanish dominion. Its riches and population are developing from day to day in an admirable manner. Its government is politico-military, exercised by a colonel. It has a well-built church of masonry at the town of Isabel Segunda.

On the southern coast, opposite the harbor of Ponce, and apparently joined to Puerto Rico by a reef, is the Caja de Muerto Island, in which there is a good anchoring ground. Its coasts abound in fish and are surrounded by keys.

To the west of Cape Rojo is the island of Mona, of volcanic origin. Its coasts rise perpendicularly to a great height above the sea level. It is inhabited by a few fishermen and abounds in goats, bulls, and swine in a wild state.

To the north-northeast of the foregoing and opposite Cape Barrionuevo is Monito Island. It is a small and elevated rock, inhabited by innumerable water fowl.

Opposite San Francisco Point is the small island of Deshecho, some 2 square kilometers in extent and covered with trees of thick foliage.

Table of distances between principal cities.

[In miles.]

Adjuntas.													
44	Aquadilla.												
24	30	Arecibo.											
60	36	66	Bayamon.										
48	130	94	28	Cayey.									
27	76	40	42	16	Coamo.								
98	104	74	38	45	61	Fajardo.							
54	140	104	38	14	26	46	Guayama.						
64	102	72	33	29	44	16	29	Humacao.					
26	17	32	69	76	60	106	78	102	Mayaguez.				
16	54	40	60	35	19	80	38	63	36	Ponce.			
25	26	33	99	63	47	108	66	91	8	28	San German.		
66	81	50	6	37	48	36	49	42	102	70	115	San Juan de Puerto Rico.	
44	20	20	17	45	24	56	44	50	54	40	54	23	Vega Baja.
18	38	38	104	52	36	97	54	79	22	16	15	82	58	Yauco.

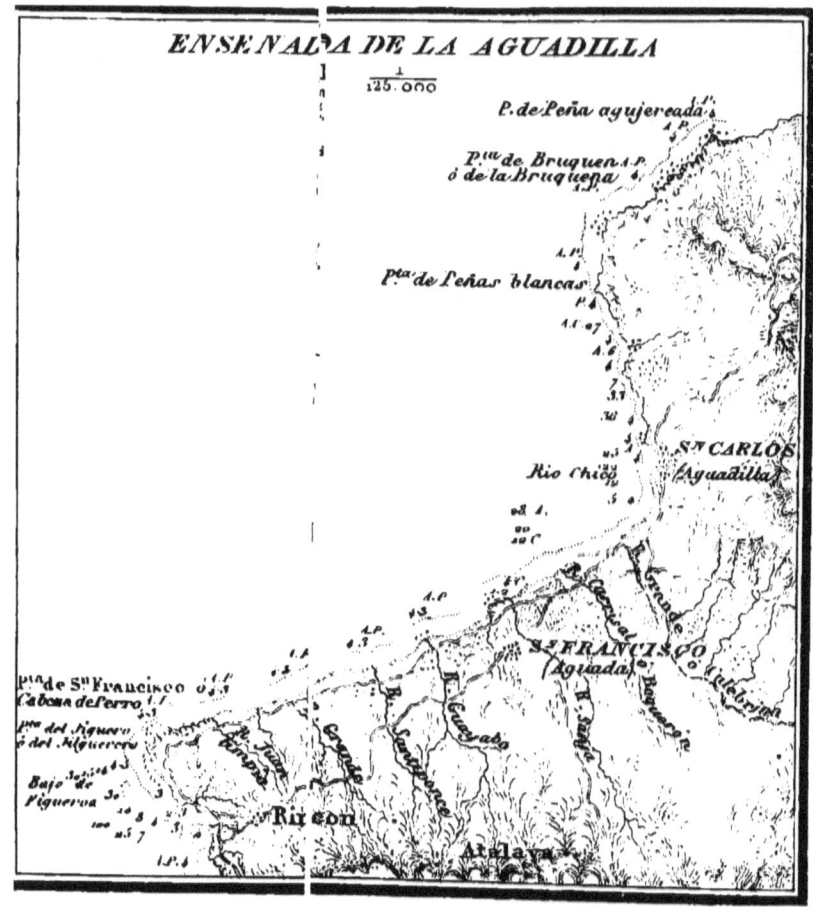

AGUA
From the
Aguadi

Good Anchorage off t
Much swell a

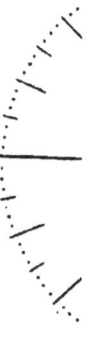

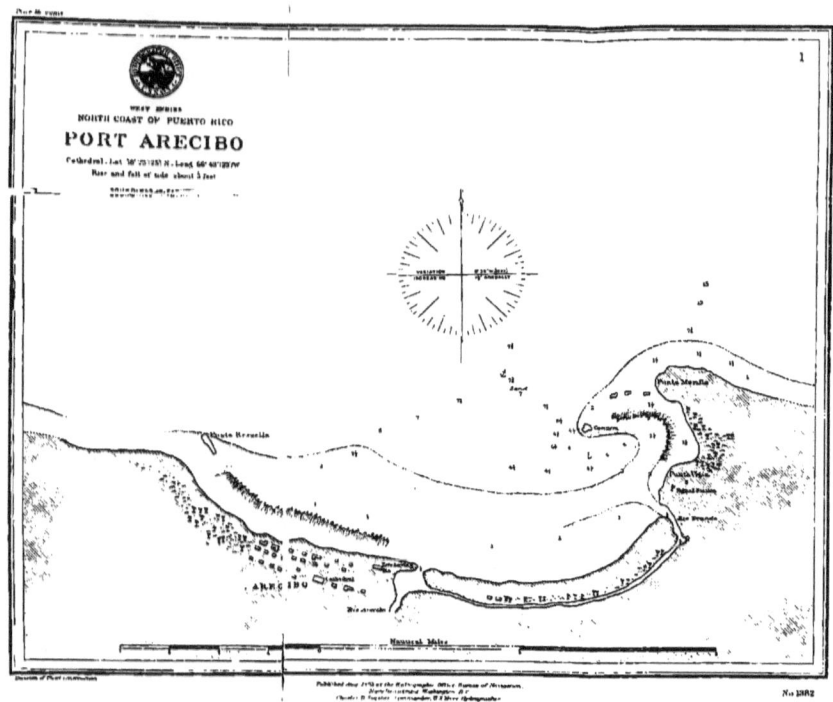

DE LA AG

$$\frac{1}{125.000}$$

P.

P.ᵗᵃ de
ó de la I.

P.ᵗᵃ de Peñas b

CITIES, TOWNS, MUNICIPAL JURISDICTIONS (AYUNTAMIENTOS), ETC.

Adjuntas.—A town of 2,320 inhabitants, with a jurisdiction numbering 18,820; situated 15½ miles from Ponce. It has a post-office and telegraph station.

Aguada.—A town of 2,563 inhabitants, with a jurisdiction numbering 9,674; situated 5 miles from Aguadilla, following the wagon road along the coast to the south. It has a post-office.

It may be considered as the oldest town on the island. It is the place where Columbus touched when, during his second voyage, he explored the island of Borinquen. Ponce de Leon also landed here with the intention of exploring and settling the island.

Aguadilla.—A city of 5,325 inhabitants, of whom 4,200 are white and 1,125 colored. The municipal jurisdiction has 16,085 inhabitants—11,100 white and 4,985 colored. It is the capital and port of the judicial district of its name, and is situated 81 miles from San Juan. The climate is hot but healthy, and there yellow fever seldom appears. It has a post-office and telegraph station.

It has one of the most picturesque aspects of any town in the country. It is situated on the shore between Cape Borinquen and Culebrinas River, at the foot of Jaicoa Mountain, stretching along in a narrow strip between the sea and the latter. The mountain is very steep, crowned with leafy trees, and on its slopes are many orange and lemon trees, palms, etc. A stream of crystalline water flows from a spring about half way up its side, and passing through Fuente, Mirador, and Comercio streets of the town, empties into the sea.

To add to the scenic beauty of the town and mountain a church rises from the mountain side near the source of the stream mentioned. It is of antique construction and has two steeples, and, although old, is in good repair; there is a bell in one steeple and a clock in the other.

The town hall is of rubble masonry and has three stories. The basement is used for a jail, the first floor for municipal offices and the telegraph station, and the second by the police forces. It was built in 1859.

The custom-house is also of masonry, one story high in front and two in the rear. The lower story is used for offices, the employees residing in the upper.

There is a small fort at the extreme north of the town which contributes to the beauty of the picture which the latter offers when seen from the sea. it is called Fort Concepción, and is armed with 11 guns.

Aguas Buenas.—A town of 1,425 inhabitants, 793 of whom are white and 632 colored. It is the chief town of a jurisdiction of 7,486 inhabitants, of whom 2,728 are white and 4,758 colored. It is situated 9 miles from Cayey. The nearest railroad station is San Juan, 24 miles distant. There is a wagon road to Caguas,

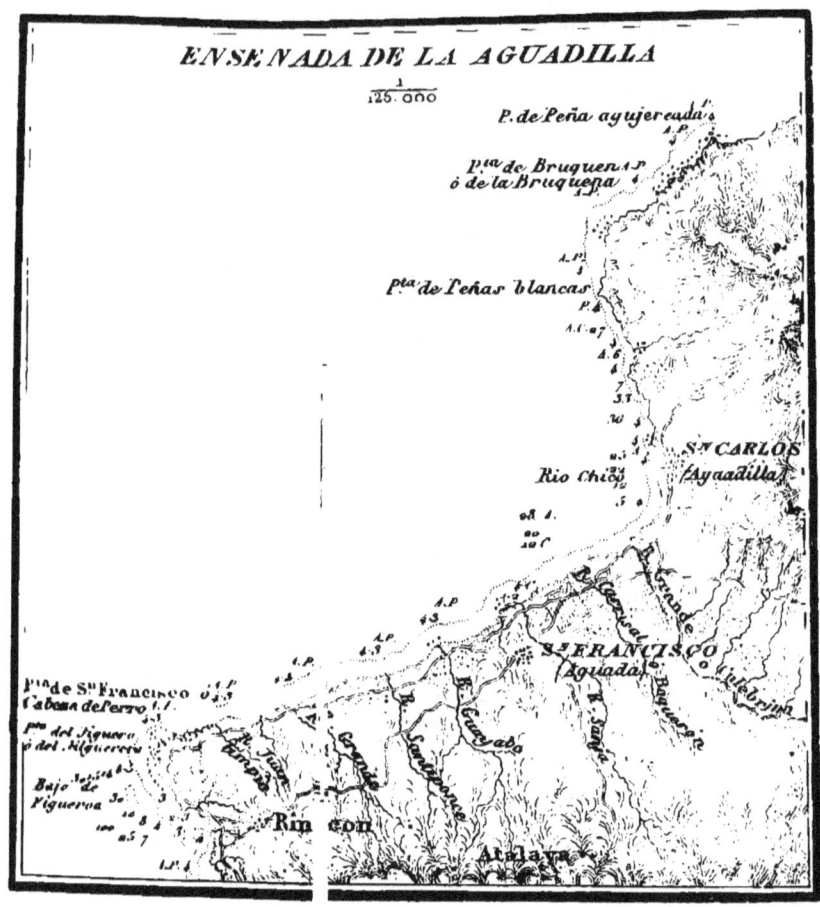

which joins the central highway. There is a telegraph station and post office.

Aibonito.—A town of 2,200 inhabitants, the chief town of a jurisdiction of 6,094 inhabitants, of whom 3,900 are white and 2,194 colored. Central highway from San Juan to Ponce. It has a post-office and telegraph station.

Añasco.—A town of 4,000 inhabitants, with a jurisdiction numbering 13,015; situated 6 miles from Mayagüez. It has a post-office and telegraph station.

Arecibo.—A town of from 6,000 to 7,000 inhabitants, with a jurisdiction numbering 29,722; it is situated on the north coast of Puerto Rico, on a peninsula formed by the sea and by the river of its name; it faces the Atlantic Ocean, and is some 50 miles distant by rail from San Juan. It is similar to all Spanish towns, with a plaza surrounded by the church and other public buildings in the center, and streets running from it in right angles, forming regular squares. The buildings are constructed of wood and brick. Its church is of naissant construction, and cost 23,000 pesos. The town hall dates from 1867; it is of rubble masonry, of two stories, and is spacious enough to accommodate a justice court, the telegraph station, and jail, and the officers belonging to the latter. The theater is of wood, but is a handsome edifice. The custom-house and the barracks of the infantry and civil guard are also of wood, but are airy and of spacious proportions. The harbor is poor, being nothing more than an open roadstead exposed to the full force of the ocean, in which vessels, during northerly winds, can hardly lie in safety. Close inshore on one side dangerous reefs stretch, a constant menace to vessels if the anchor does not hold. Into this harbor empties a narrow and shallow stream called the Rio Grande de Arecibo. Goods are conveyed on this river to and from the town in flat-bottomed boats, with the aid of long poles and by dint of much pushing and patience. At the bar of the river everything is again transferred into lighters, and thence to vessels. It is a tedious and expensive process. However, Arecibo is quite an important port. The want of good roads in the island makes such a place as Arecibo far more important than it would naturally be. There is a railroad to San Juan, and a post-office and telegraph station.

The environs are extremely picturesque, and have a peculiar feature which renders them worthy of a visit. About $7\frac{1}{4}$ miles southeast of the town, in the place called "El Concejo," there is a rock about 108 yards high, cut off vertically. About one-third the way up from the bottom is the entrance to a grotto, covered with brambles, and about $1\frac{1}{2}$ yards high by 3 wide. It has a number of caverns and arches, stalactites, and wonderful curiosities, etc., peculiar to caves generally.

The whole valley of the Arecibo is picturesque. Descending from the mountain of Utuado the whole course of the river presents itself to the view. On either side of its voluminous course are a number of streams forming beautiful cascades, and, while

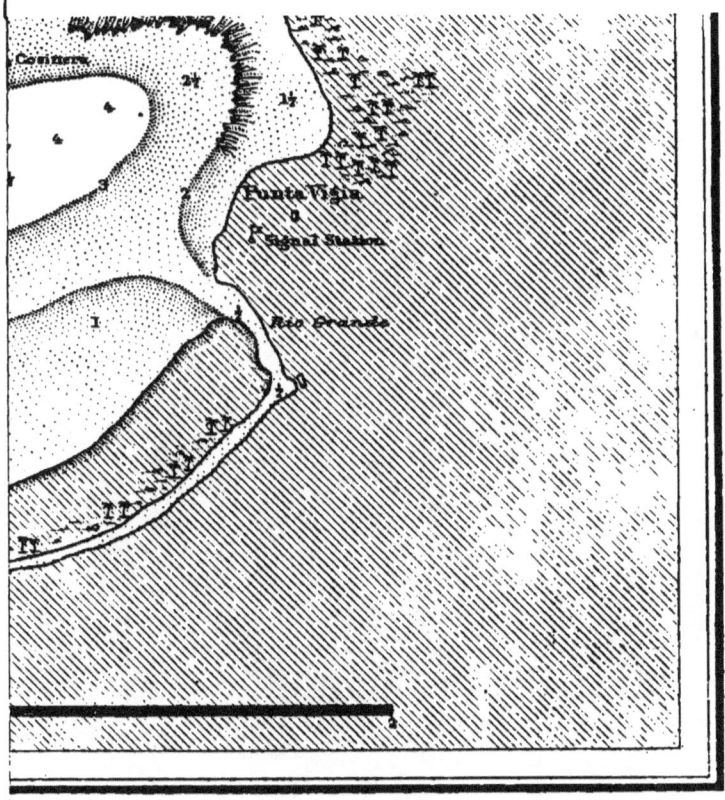

No. 1382

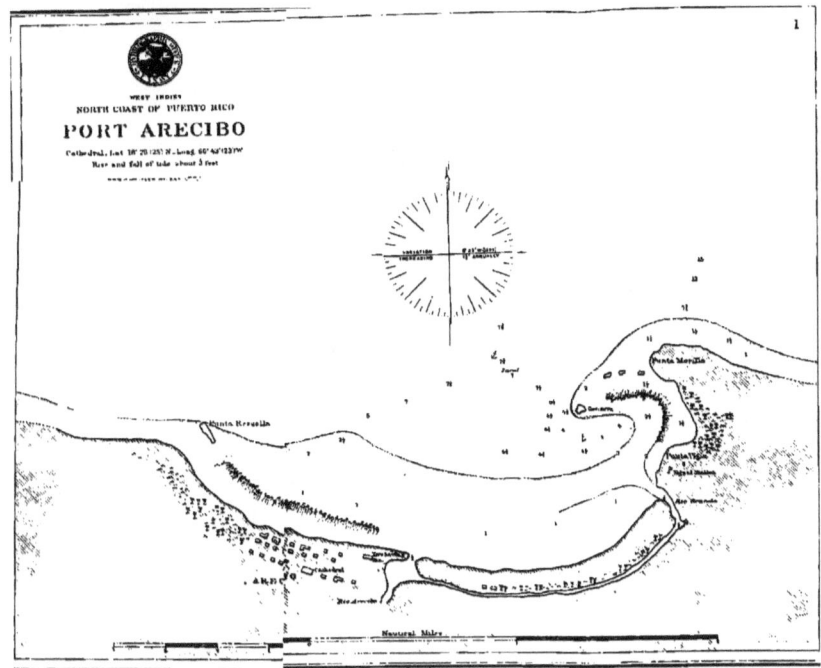

delighting the traveler, they also serve to irrigate the intermediate valleys which extend to the river. The latter becomes obstructed at the farther end and grows sluggish, its waters during freshets overflowing both banks and fertilizing the land for pastures, which are always covered with cattle, mules, and horses, the best on the island. In the center of these meadows are seen the homes of the landowners, surrounded by the leafy banana trees, tall palms, and some sugar, coffee, and cotton plantations. The limits of each proprietor are marked by barriers of orange, lemon, and other trees which the fertile land produces in exquisite variety, the result being the most delightful and charming country imaginable.

Arroyo.—Arroyo, in the judicial district of Guayama (southeast portion), is a small seaport of about 1,200 inhabitants. It was founded in 1885. The annual exports to the United States average 7,000 to 10,000 heads of sugar, 2,000 to 5,000 casks of molasses, and 50 to 150 casks and barrels of bay rum. Its jurisdiction has 5,644 inhabitants. It is situated 5 miles from Guayama and $54\frac{1}{2}$ from San Juan. It has a post-office.

It is one of the brightest looking towns on the island, not only on account of its handsome harbor, but the aspect of its houses, almost all of which are of wood and surrounded by gardens. The church, which has two steeples, is small but very pretty.

The caves of Aguas Buenas, situated in the Sumidero ward, have a curious feature; they run under the Cagüitas River, a distance of over 400 yards. There are three of them, called, respectively, Oscura, Clara, and Ermita.

Barceloneta.—A town of 1,000 inhabitants, with a jurisdiction numbering 7,000, situated on the north coast of the province. It has a railroad station and a post-office.

Barranquitas.—A town of 688 inhabitants—404 white and 284 colored. Chief town of a jurisdiction of 6,754 inhabitants, of whom 4,282 are white and 2,472 colored. It has a post-office. The nearest railroad station is Cantaño, $28\frac{1}{4}$ miles distant.

Barros.—A town of 650 inhabitants, of whom 421 are white and 229 colored. It is the chief town of a jurisdiction of 13,000 inhabitants, and is situated 31 miles from Ponce. It has a post-office and telegraph station.

Bayamón.—A town of 2,500 inhabitants, with a jurisdiction numbering 15,167, situated 6 miles from San Juan. There is a belt line railroad and one to San Juan. There is a post-office and telegraph station. It is the capital of the principal department of the island, and is 5 miles from the north coast, south of the capital, and has east of it the town of Rio Piedras, which is connected with San Juan by a steam tramway. It was founded in 1772, and is now a rich and important place. Its principal streets are those of Puerto Rico, Comercio, and La Palma. The town hall has two stories, is built of rubble masonry, and has connected with it a barracks and jail.

Cabo Rojo.—A town of 2,735 inhabitants, of whom 1,702 are white and 1,033 colored. It is the chief town of a jurisdiction of 16,775 inhabitants, and is situated 8 miles from San German. It has a post-office and telegraph station.

Caguas.—A town of 4,340 inhabitants, of whom 1,536 are white and 2,804 colored. It is the chief town of a jurisdiction of 15,129 inhabitants, 6,824 white and 8,305 colored. There is a post-office and a telegraph station.

Camuy.—A town of 956 inhabitants, 750 white and 206 colored. Chief town of a jurisdiction of 10,342 inhabitants, of whom 9,863 are white and 479 colored. It is situated 9¼ miles from Arecibo. There is a railroad station, a telegraph station, and a post-office.

Carolina.—A town of 5,052 inhabitants, with a jurisdiction numbering 10,919, situated 25 kilometers from San Juan. There is a local highway and a post-office and telegraph station.

Cayey.—A town of 3,895 inhabitants, of whom 2,700 are white and 1,195 colored. It is the chief town of a jurisdiction of 14,257 inhabitants, 9,500 white and 4,757 colored. It is situated 37 miles from San Juan and 14 from Guayama. Wagon road from San Juan to Ponce. The nearest railroad station is Caguas. There is a post-office and telegraph station.

Ceiba.—A town of 744 inhabitants, with a jurisdiction numbering 4,142, situated 17 miles from Humacao. There is a wagon road to Fajardo and Naguabo. It has a post-office.

Ciales.—A town and jurisdiction of 15,000 inhabitants, situated 19 miles from Arecibo. It has a post-office.

Cidra.—A town of 2,400 inhabitants, with a jurisdiction numbering 8,000, situated 6 miles from Cayey. It has a post-office.

Coamo.—A village of 2,206 inhabitants, with a jurisdiction numbering 10,482. It is the capital of the judicial district of its name. There is a telegraph station.

Comeiro (formerly Sabana del Palmar).—A municipal jurisdiction of 6,650 inhabitants, situated 17 miles from San Juan. It has a post-office.

Corozal.—A town and jurisdiction of 11,551 inhabitants, situated 22 miles from San Juan. It has a post-office and telegraph station.

Dorado.—A town of 3,985 inhabitants, with a jurisdiction numbering 3,985; situated 4¾ miles from San Juan. It has a railroad station, post-office, and telegraph station.

Fajardo.—A town of 3,376 inhabitants, of whom 1,776 are white and 1,600 colored. It is the chief town of a jurisdiction of 8,779 inhabitants, of whom 4,891 are white and 3,888 colored. It is situated 15¼ miles from Humacao on the east coast of the island. The port is handsome, with a third-class light-house at the entrance at the point called Cabezas de San Juan, and a custom-house open to universal commerce. The town is about 1¼ miles from the bay. The only important industry of the district is the manufacture of muscovado sugar, to which most of the planters devote themselves. Shooks, hickory hoops, pine boards, and provisions come from the United States in considerable quantities. Sugar and molasses are exported, and occasionally tortoise shell.

PUERTO DE GUANICA.
South Side of Porto Rico.
From a Spanish Government Survey in 1875.

1

The climate is temperate and healthy. It has a post-office and telegraph station. It dates from 1774.

Its church is of masonry, with a steeple with clock and bell, and was built in 1895, at which date the town hall was also built. This town was besieged on November 14, 1824, by Commodore Porter, but the inhabitants showed such a disposition to resist that he put to sea again.

Two conflagrations, in April of 1832 and 1833, respectively, destroyed a large part of the town, which, however, is to-day visibly progressing just as the others of the island.

Guanica.—A small town of 1,000 inhabitants, on southern coast, about 6 miles south of Yauco, of which city it forms the port, and with which it is connected by a good road practicable in dry weather. It is situated on the Bay of Guanica, which is one of the best ports in the whole island. The banks to the right are steep and form a good natural wharf. Three vessels can lie alongside and unload by means of gang plank. Vessels of 30 feet draft can easily enter bay and proceed close inshore. No fortifications or mines.

Guayama.—A village of 4,500 inhabitants, with a jurisdiction numbering 12,884. It is the chief town of the judicial district of its name, and is situated on the south coast 49 miles from San Juan. It has a telephone, a railroad station, a post-office, and a telegraph station. It was founded in 1736.

Its church is one of the finest on the island, being rich in altars and ornaments. It was constructed in 1873, with 20 yards front by 44 deep, and it cost 49,000 pesos. The town hall is a good building of two stories, of which the upper is occupied by the offices of the municipal council, and the lower by the telegraph station and police quarters.

Guayanilla.—A town of 600 inhabitants, with a jurisdiction numbering 7,833, situated 14 miles from Ponce. It is a seaport, and has a post-office and telegraph station. There is a wagon road to Ponce, Yauco, and Peñuelas.

Gurabo.—A town of 870 inhabitants, with a jurisdiction numbering 6,366. It has a post-office and telegraph station.

Hatillo.—A town of 416 inhabitants, chief town of a jurisdiction of 9,140 inhabitants, situated 54½ miles from San Juan and 5½ miles from Arecibo. It has a post-office.

Hato Grande.—A town of 1,994 inhabitants, with a jurisdiction numbering 12,618, situated 19 miles from Cayey. There is a post-office and telegraph station.

Hormigueros.—A town and jurisdiction of 3,023 inhabitants, situated 7¼ miles from San German. It has a post-office and telegraph station.

Humacao.—A village of 5,765 inhabitants, with a jurisdiction numbering 14,726, situated 47 miles from San Juan. It is a department capital and capital of the judicial district of its name. The nearest railroad station is Naguabo. There is a post-office and telegraph station.

This village, founded in 1793, is about 3 miles from the coast on the river of its name. It has a spacious and beautiful square, which, together with its church, ranks among the first in the island. The church is of modern construction, having been finished in 1877 at a cost of 48,000 pesos.

The town hall and jail constitute a good building of masonry, in which are located also the municipal court and the guard corps. It was finished in 1849, and its cost was 26,470 pesos. The barracks and the hospital of San Vicente de Paul are also handsome buildings of masonry, the former built in 1862 and the latter in 1867.

Isabela.—A municipal jurisdiction of 12,502 inhabitants, situated 10½ miles from Aguadilla. It has good buildings of modern construction. There is a wagon road to Aguadilla and Quebradillas. There is a post-office.

Juana Diaz.—A village and municipal jurisdiction of 21,032 inhabitants. It is situated 8 miles from Ponce and 72 miles from San Juan. It has a post-office and railroad station.

Juncos.—A municipal jurisdiction of 7,282 inhabitants. There is a post-office and telegraph station.

Lares.—A municipal jurisdiction of 17,020 inhabitants, of whom 15,005 are white and 2,015 colored. Población is the chief ward of the jurisdiction, with 1,575 inhabitants, situated 24 miles from Aguadilla. There is a wagon road to Aguadilla, Arecibo, and Mayagüez. There is a market every Sunday; there are casinos, a municipal library, and a post-office.

Las Marias.—A town of 750 inhabitants, with a jurisdiction numbering 9,700; situated 15½ miles from Mayagüez. It has two theaters and two casinos. The nearest railroad station is in the ward of Naranjales, at a distance of 6 miles. There is a post-office and telegraph station.

Loiza.—A town of 907 inhabitants, chief town of a jurisdiction of 9,561; situated 19 miles from San Juan. The nearest railroad station is Rio Piedras, 19 miles distant. It has a post-office.

Luquillo.—A town of 1,560 inhabitants, with a jurisdiction numbering 6,893; situated 31 miles from Humacao. Gold exists in the sands of its rivers. The nearest railroad station is Carolina, 19 miles distant. It has a post-office.

Manati.—A town and jurisdiction of 11,967 inhabitants, situated 17 miles from Arecibo. There is a railroad station, a post-office, and a telegraph station.

Maricao.—A municipal jurisdiction of 8,000 inhabitants, situated 9½ miles from San German and 15½ from Mayagüez. There is a wagon road to Mayagüez and Las Marias.

Maunabo.—A town of 903 inhabitants, of whom 346 are white and 567 colored. It is the chief town of a jurisdiction of 5,689 inhabitants—1,495 white and 4,194 colored. It is situated 24 miles from Guayama. There is a post-office and telegraph station.

Mayagüez.—A city of 11,615 inhabitants, with a jurisdiction numbering 28,026. The majority of the population is white. It is the third city in importance of the island, being situated in the

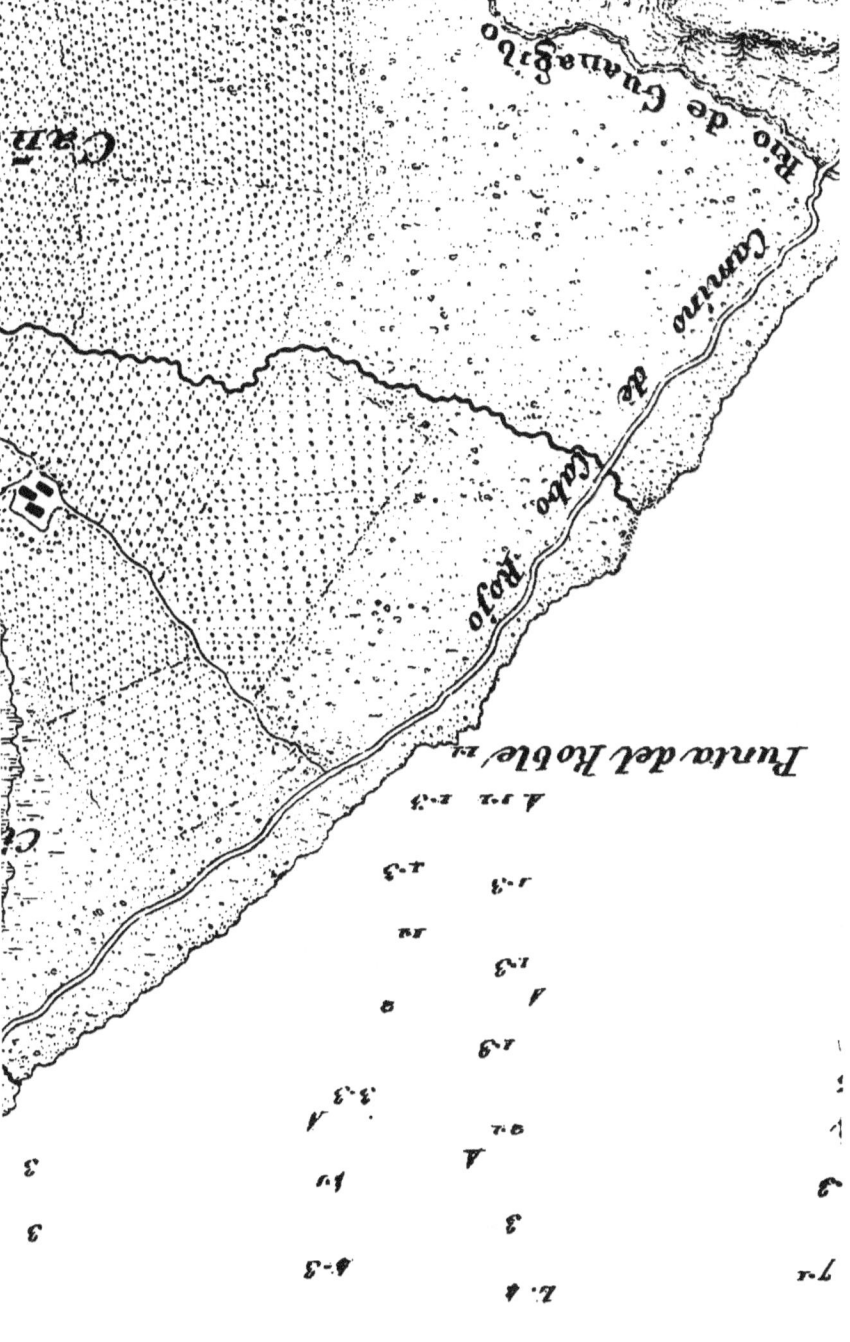

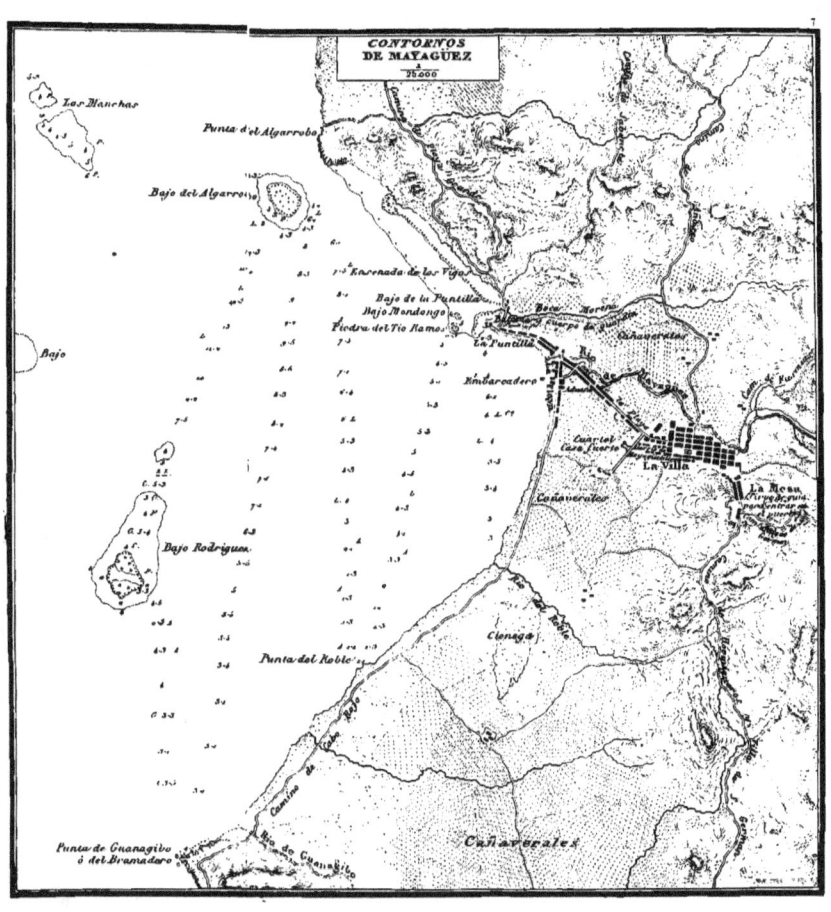

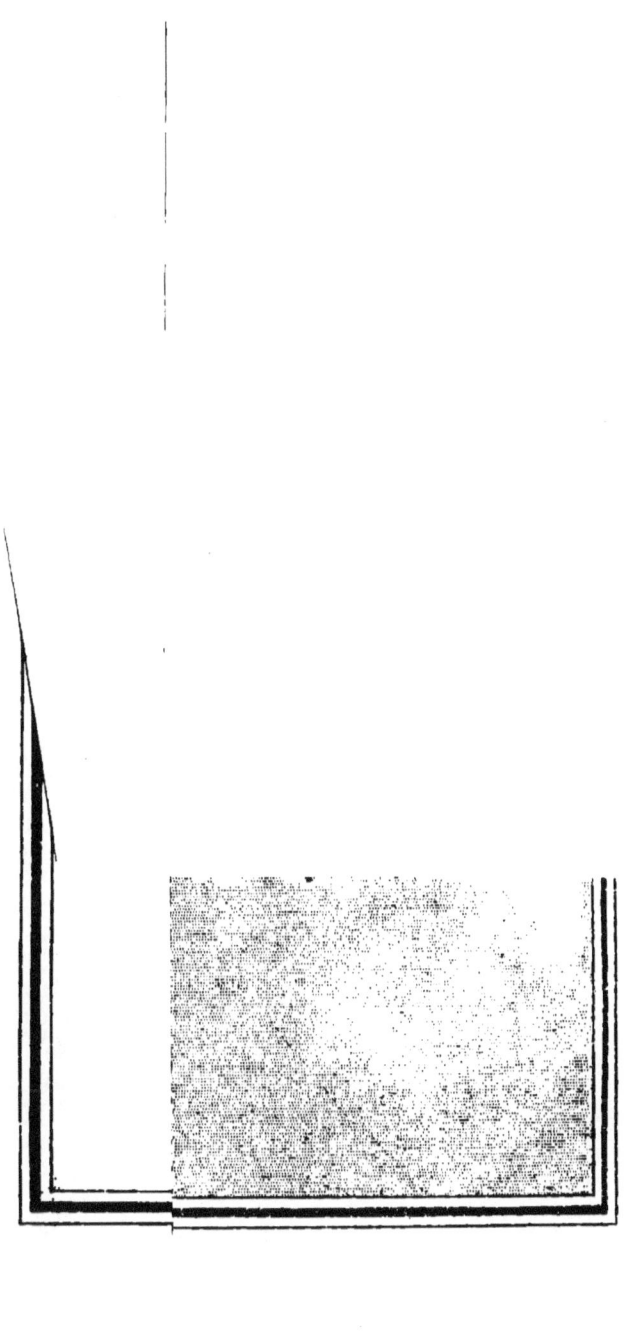

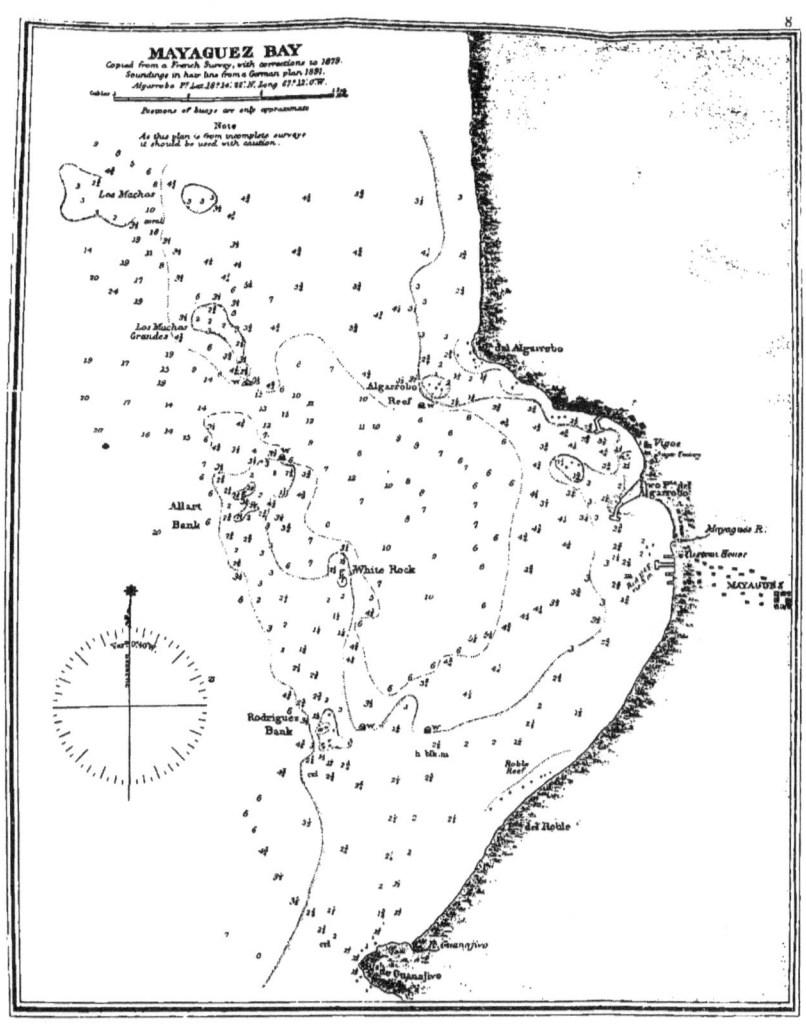

TARY INFORMATION DIVISION.

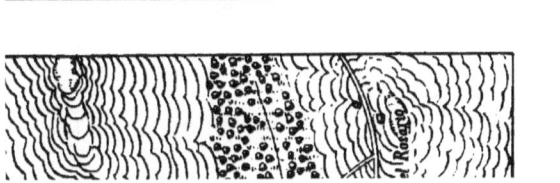

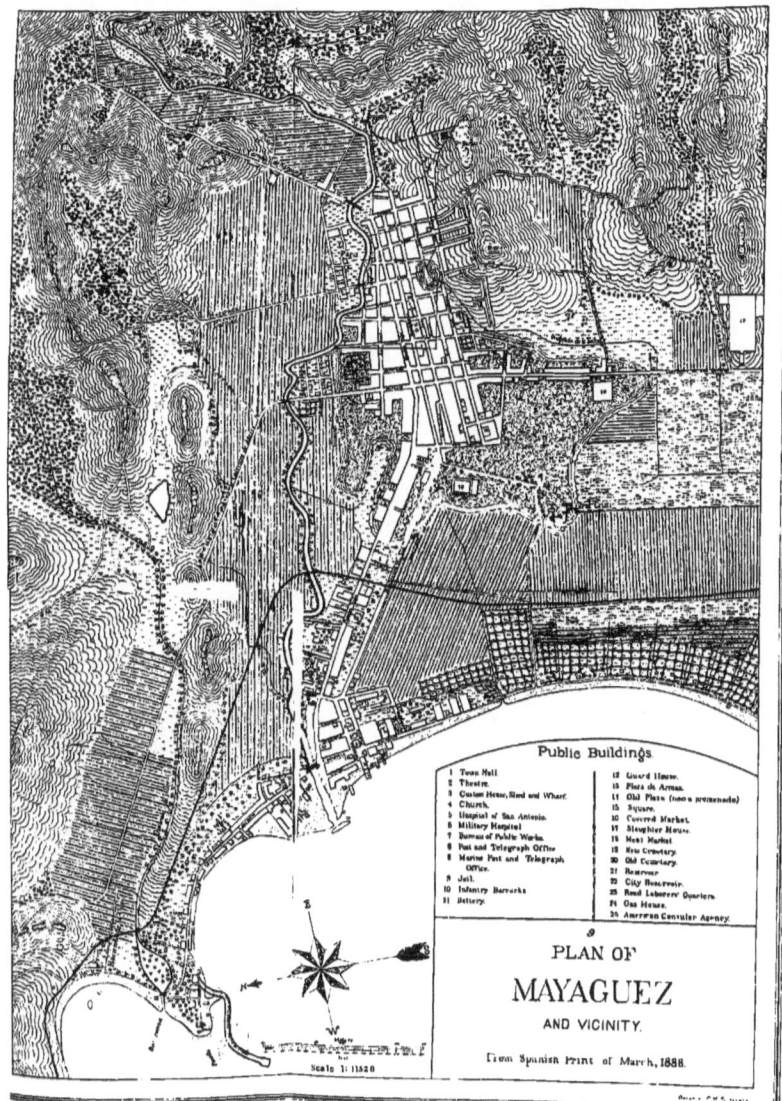

west part, facing what is generally known as the "Mona Channel." It is a seaport of considerable commerce, and is 102 miles from San Juan. Of industry there is little to be said, except that there are three manufactories of chocolate, which is for local consumption. Sugar, coffee, oranges, pineapples, and cocoanuts are exported largely, all except coffee principally to the United States. Of sugar the muscovado goes to the United States and the centrifugal to Spain. Mayagüez is the second port for coffee, the average annual export being 170,000 hundredweights. The quality is of the best, ranging in price with Java and other first-rate brands. The lower grades are sent to Cuba. About 50,000 bags of flour are imported into this port every year from the United States out of the 180,000 bags that are consumed in the whole island. The climate is excellent, the temperature never exceeding 90° F. The city is connected by tramway with the neighboring towns of Aguadilla, and a railroad is being constructed to Lares, one of the largest interior towns. It has a civil and military hospital, two asylums, a public library, three bridges, a handsome market, constructed of iron, a slaughter-house, recently constructed, a theater, etc., and a number of societies of instruction, recreation, and commerce. It has a post-office and telegraph station. It was founded in 1760, was given the title of villa (village) in 1836, and that of city in 1877.

On the east and south it is bounded by the Hormigueros Mountains, on the north by those of Añasco, and on the west by the sea. The part comprised by the vega (plain) is very fertile, and here are grown all fruits of the island. The river, called also Mayagüez, has not much water and divides the town in two parts. Its sands formerly yielded much gold, but to-day hardly any is found. The town is large, handsome, and very modern. There are no less than 37 streets and 3 squares—the Principal, the Mercado, and Iglesia—all adorned by pretty fountains. Two iron bridges called, respectively, Marina and Guenar, connect the two parts of the town. The former is some 33 yards long by 8 wide and was built in 1877, at a cost of 12,000 pesos. That of Guenar is only 19 yards long by 5 wide. It was finished in 1872 and cost 3,791 pesos.

The church was built in 1760. It is of masonry, with two steeples and good altars. The town hall, situated on Principal square, is a good stone building of three stories. It has in it, besides the offices of the municipal council, the jail and telegraph station. It is a modern structure, was finished in 1845, and cost 25,000 pesos. Annexed to it is the Casa del Rey, built in 1832, and serving for offices of the military commandancy.

The infantry barracks is also a building of modern construction, dating from 1848, and, though of simple architecture, it is very capacious. It has accommodations for lodging eight companies and has quarters for the chief and his aids, as well as other necessary arrangements.

Among the buildings devoted to charity are the military hospital and the San Antonio Asylum. The former is of masonry, two stories high, and owned by private parties. The second owes its origin to the charity of Antonio Blanés, who in 1865 donated this instruction to Mayagüez, since which time it has been maintained by the charity of the inhabitants.

The Spanish ultramarine bureau, the public library, and the casino are deserving of a visit on account of the fine decorations of their rooms.

The market is the best on the island. It is constructed of iron and stone and covers an area of over 1,500 square yards. It cost 70,000 pesos. About 7 miles from Mayagüez, across a rough and mountainous country, is the sanctuary of Montserrate. This wild-looking place is visited by many who go there as pilgrims, and many legends and traditions are told concerning it.

The church is on top of a mountain. It is of masonry, quite capacious, and of agreeable aspect. From here is seen the most fertile and beautiful plain on the island, watered by the Juanajibos and Boquerón rivers and inclosed by high mountain ridges, which send forth multitudes of streams, the plain being bounded by the sea and having in it the towns of Cabo Rojo and San German.

Moco.—Village of 1,034 inhabitants, with a jurisdiction numbering 11,084, situated 4¼ miles from the station of Aguadilla, with which it is connected by a wagon road. There is a post-office.

Mororis.—A town of 619 inhabitants, with a jurisdiction numbering 8,234, situated 32 miles from Arecibo. It has a post-office.

Naguabo.—A town of 2,384 inhabitants, with a jurisdiction numbering 9,876, situated 9¼ miles from Humacao, on the east side of the island; one of the best seaports of the island. It is the place where Columbus first arrived. It has a post-office and telegraph station. It was founded anew in 1821, because the town of this name situated in another locality had been destroyed. It has a handsome square with a fountain in its center, a church of masonry with two steeples, a town hall, and a hospital of wood.

Naranjito.—A municipal jurisdiction of 5,825 inhabitants, situated 21 miles from San Juan.

Patillas.—A municipal jurisdiction of 10,553 inhabitants, situated 62 miles from Guayama. It has a post-office.

Peñuelas.—A town of 859 inhabitants, with a jurisdiction numbering 10,623 inhabitants, situated 10 miles from Ponce.

Piedras.—A town of 1,200 inhabitants, of whom 900 are white and 300 colored. It is the chief town of a jurisdiction of 8,545 inhabitants, 5,698 white and 2,847 colored. It is situated 3¾ miles from Humacao, on the highway from San Juan to Humacao. There is a post-office.

Ponce.—A city of 22,000 inhabitants, with a jurisdiction numbering 47,000. It is situated on the south coast of the island, on a plain, about 2 miles from the seaboard. It is the chief town of the judicial district of its name, and is 70 miles from San Juan.

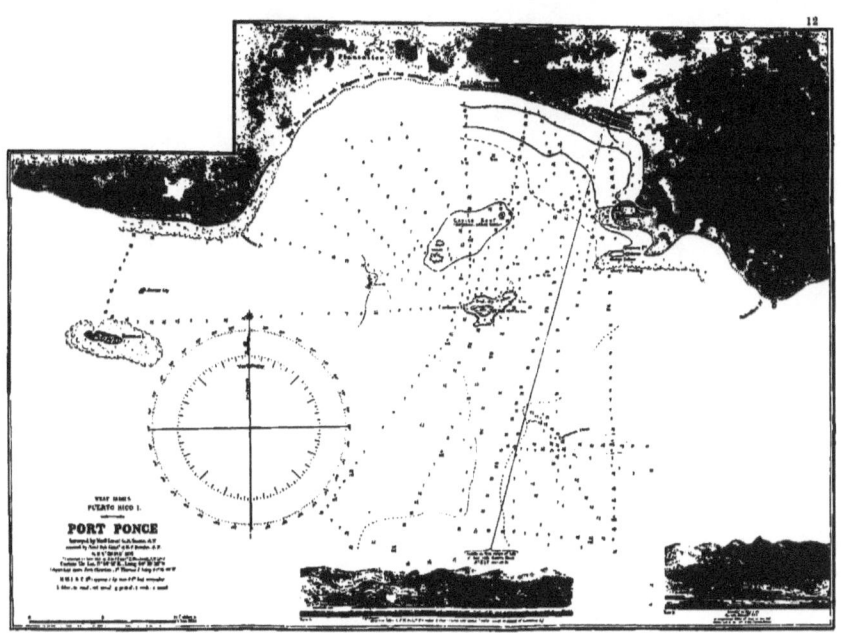

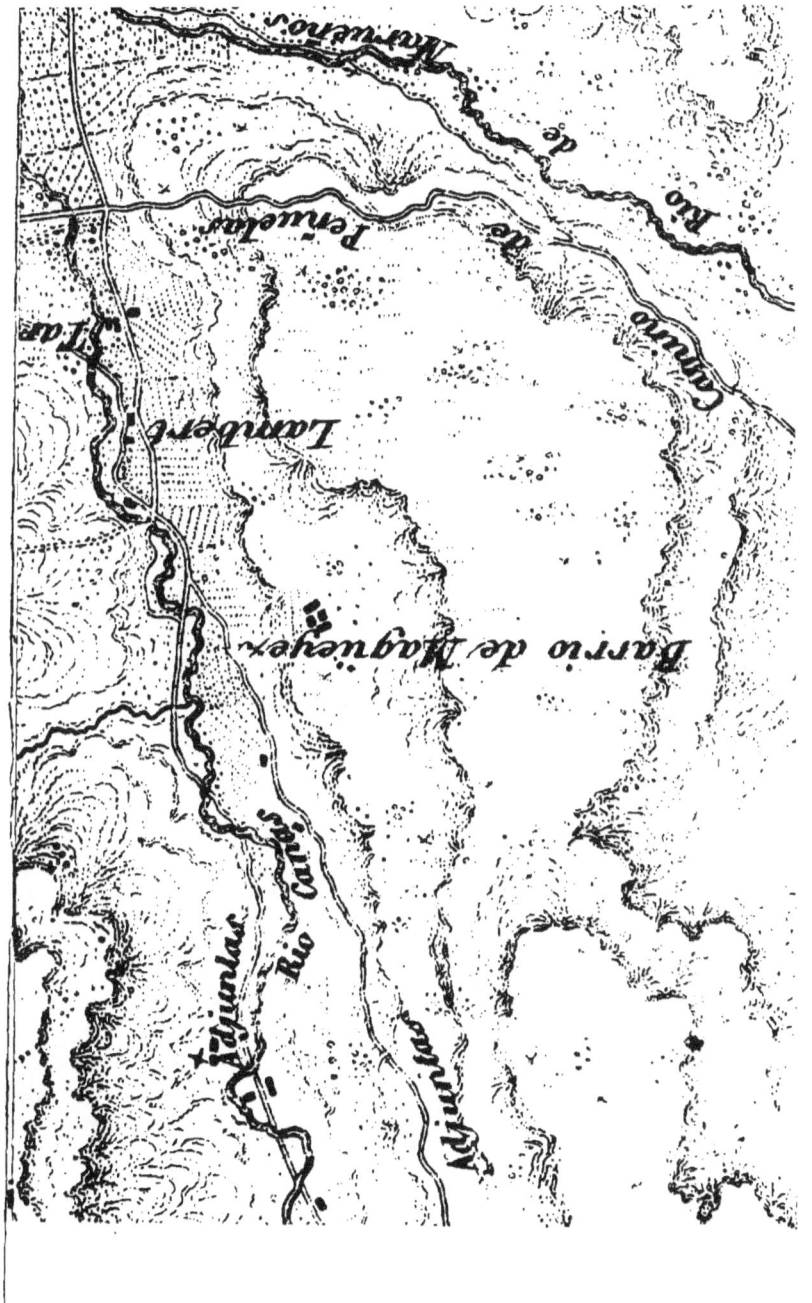

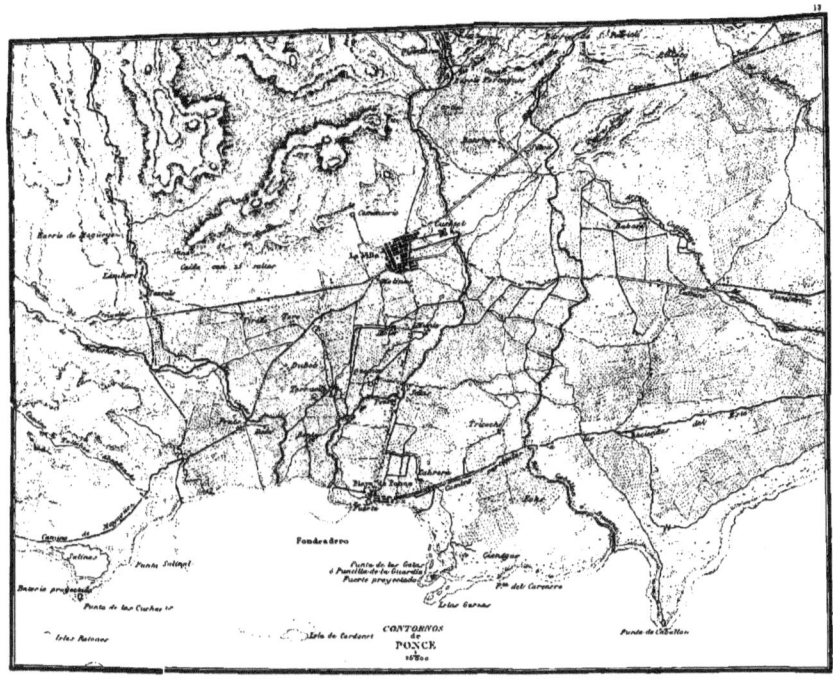

It is regularly built, the central part almost exclusively of brick houses and the suburbs of wood. It is the residence of the military commander, and the seat of an official chamber of commerce. There is an appellate criminal court, besides other courts; 2 churches, one Protestant, said to be the only one in the Spanish West Indies; 2 hospitals besides the military hospital, a home of refuge for old and poor, 2 cemeteries, 3 asylums, several casinos, 3 theaters, a market, a municipal public library, 3 first-class hotels, 3 barracks, a park, gas works, a perfectly equipped fire department, a bank, thermal and natural baths, etc. Commercially, Ponce is the second city of importance on the island. A fine road leads to the port (Playa), where all the import and export trade is transacted. Playa has about 5,000 inhabitants, and here are situated the custom-house, the office of the captain of the port, and all the consular offices. The port is spacious and will hold vessels of 25 feet draft. The climate, on account of the sea breezes during the day and land breezes at night, is not oppressive, but very hot and dry; and, as water for all purposes, including the fire department, is amply supplied by an aqueduct 4,442 yards long, it is said that the city of Ponce is perhaps the healthiest place in the whole island. There is a stagecoach to San Juan, Mayagüez, Guayama, etc. There is a railroad to Yauco, a post-office, and a telegraph station.

It is believed that Ponce was founded in 1600; it was given the title of villa in 1848, and in 1877 that of city. Of its 34 streets the best are Mayor, Salud, Villa, Vives, Marina, and Comercio. The best squares are Principal and Las Delicias, which are separated by the church of Nuestra Señora de Guadalupe. The church, as old as the town itself, began to be reconstructed in 1838 and was finished in 1847. It is 86 yards long by 43 broad, and has two steeples, rich altars, and fine ornaments.

The Protestant church is of gothic architecture, of galvanized iron outside and wood within; it was built in 1874.

The town hall, which also serves as a jail, is a good two-story building of masonry, and was finished in 1877. There are two barracks, one for infantry, with a capacity for 700 men, and another for cavalry. The former was constructed in 1849, and is two stories high, while the latter is a one-story structure belonging to the municipal council.

The military hospital, of masonry, is situated on Castillo street, and has a capacity for 70 patients.

The smallpox and pestilential hospitals are more simple and are situated outside the city limits.

The albergue de Tricoche (hospital) was built with money left by Valentin Tricoche for this purpose in 1863. It is in the northern part of the town, is built of masonry on the doric order, with a porch supported by doric columns. It has a capacity for 60 persons.

The Damas Asylum is built of masonry, with an elegant porch, iron gate, and garden at its entrance. It is maintained by money left by various persons and by other charitable means, and will accommodate 12 men and 12 women, having, besides, 4 beds designed for sick seamen.

The theater is called the Pearl, and it deserves this name, for it is the finest on the island. It has a sculptured porch, on the Byzantine order, with very graceful columns. It is mostly built of iron and marble and cost over 70,000 pesos. It is 52 yards deep by 29 wide. The inside is beautiful, the boxes and seats roomy and nicely decorated. It may, by a mechanical arrangement, be converted into a dancing hall.

About $1\frac{1}{8}$ miles northeast of the town are the Quintana thermal baths, in a building surrounded by pretty gardens. They are visited by sufferers from rheumatism and various other diseases.

The city of Ponce proper has no military defenses, but in the hills to the north of the town a series of earth intrenchments have lately been constructed. West of Ponce, where the railroad and military road touch the shore, earthworks have been constructed to guard this strategic point. There are about 30 mountain howitzers in Ponce available for defense of the city and the railroad.

Quebradillas.—A town of 1,055 inhabitants—868 white and 187 colored. Chief town of a jurisdiction of 5,899 inhabitants, of whom 3,520 are white and 379 colored. It is situated $17\frac{1}{2}$ miles from Aguadilla. It has a post-office.

Rincon.—A town of 300 inhabitants, with a jurisdiction numbering 5,817, situated 15 miles from Mayagüez. There is a railroad station and a post-office.

Rio Grande.—A town of 695 inhabitants, of whom 220 are white and 475 colored. It is the chief town of a jurisdiction of 6,170 inhabitants, 2,462 of whom are white and 3,726 colored. The town has 8 wards. It is situated 25 miles from San Juan. The nearest railroad station is Luquillo, 27 kilometers distant. There is a post-office.

Rio Piedras.—A town of 1,054 inhabitants—581 white and 473 colored. It is the chief town of a jurisdiction of 9,010 inhabitants, of whom 3,482 are white and 5,528 colored. It is situated 7 miles from San Juan, with which it is connected by a railroad. It has a theater and a casa de recreo for the governors of the province. There is a post-office and telegraph station.

Its church was built in 1831 and has since received important repairs and improvements. It has 2 towers, is well proportioned, and finely ornamented.

Sabana Grande.—A municipal jurisdiction of 9,587 inhabitants, situated 18 miles from Mayagüez. It is on the highway from Mayagüez to Ponce. There is a post-office.

Salinas.—A town of 655 inhabitants, with a jurisdiction numbering 4,104 inhabitants, situated 22 miles from Cayey and 12 miles from Guayama. It has a good harbor a short distance from town.

San German.—A city of 8,000 inhabitants, with a jurisdiction numbering 30,600; it is situated 115 miles from San Juan. It has

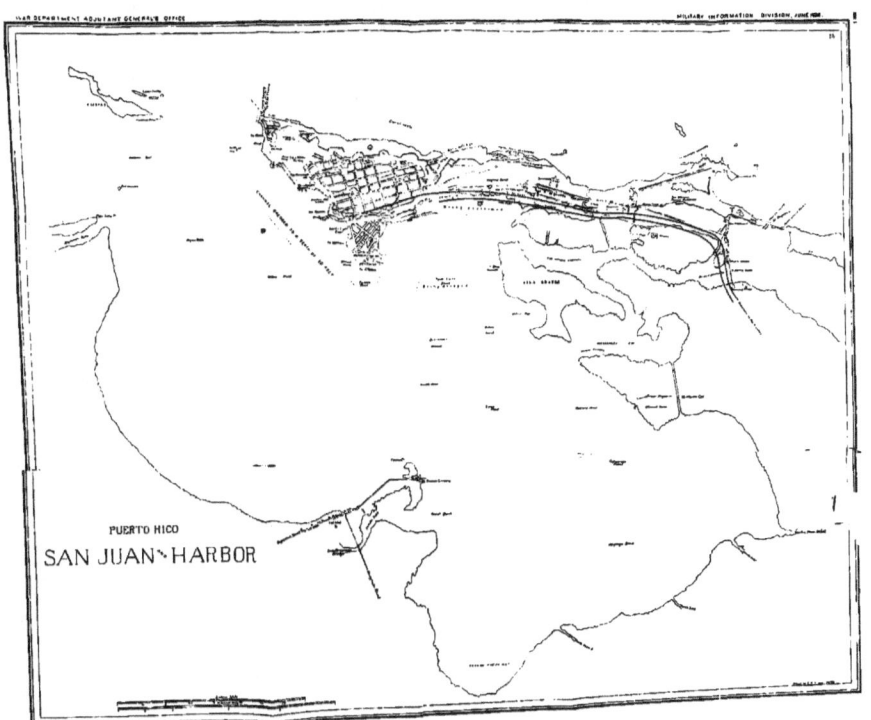

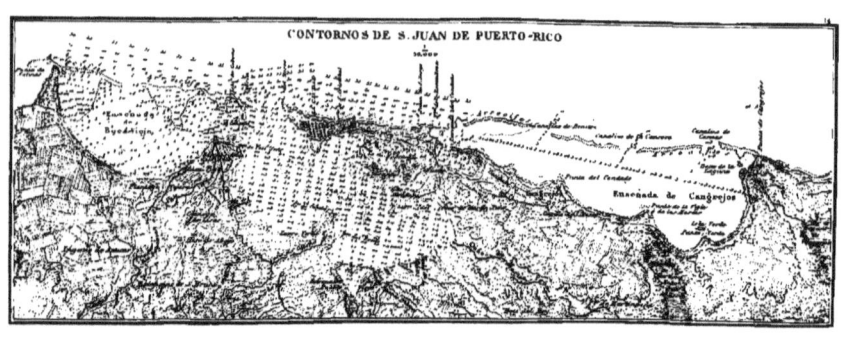

RTO-RICO

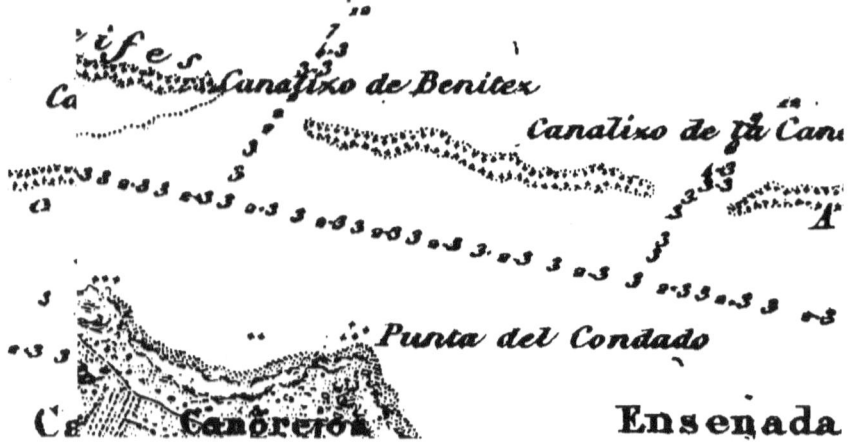

3 magnificent market places, a charity hospital, a seminary, good school buildings, theater, casino, etc. There is a railroad in construction, and a post-office and telegraph station.

It is situated on a long, uneven hill, at the foot of which lies the beautiful valley of the Juanajibos and Boquerón rivers, which is made a beautiful garden by the orange, lemon, and tamarind trees, and various other plants growing here. Coffee, cotton, and cane are also raised.

The town was founded in 1511 by Capt. Miguel Toro, and has enjoyed the title of city since 1877. Its principal streets are called Luna and Comercio. Its chief plaza is square and large in size; its church is quite regular and of old construction. There are two hospitals—one for men and one for women. The town hall is a good building, of masonry, two stories high, with a clock tower. Finally, the institution of second-grade instruction and the barracks of the infantry and civil guard merit mention.

The inhabitants of San German have always been distinguished for their great love of country. When the English landed there in 1743 they were soon repulsed and driven off, with the loss of one vessel. Many persons have distinguished themselves for their bravery and patriotism.

San Juan.—San Juan, the capital, is situated on the northern coast, on a long and narrow island, separated from the main island, at one end, by a shallow arm of the sea, over which is the bridge of San Antonio, connecting it with the mainland, which runs out at this point in a long sand spit, some 9 miles in length, apparently to meet the smaller islands. At the other end the island ends in a rugged bluff or promontory some hundred feet high and three-fourths of a mile distant from the main island.

This promontory is crowned by Morro Castle, the principal fortification of the town. The form of the castle is that of an obtuse angle, with three tiers of batteries, placed one above the other, toward the sea, their fires crossing each other. Toward the city it has a wall, flanked by two bastions of heavy artillery, which dominates all of the intermediate space, which has the name of Morro, and also part of the city and the north shore of the sea. It has the usual barracks, large water tanks, warehouses, chapel, and the necessary offices—all bombproof. A mine descends from it to the seashore, through the entrance of the port, its issue being defended by a battery. This enables troops to enter and leave the castle, to receive succor, etc.

The site occupied by this important fortification was always regarded with preference by persons charged with the execution of works of defense for the town. It was originally only a battery, but the importance of the point being soon realized, in 1584 the plan of the fortress was drawn, and it has been gradually developed until it has reached its present stage of perfection.

There is a revolving light-house placed on the top of the castle, rising to a height of 170 feet above the level of the sea.

At the western end of the island on which San Juan is situated

1676——3

is the entrance to the harbor. On the right bank is the castle of San Juan de la Cruz, situated on the Ceñedo shoal, which is very dangerous during a north wind. The channel is narrow, with a rocky bottom, so close under the headland that one can almost leap ashore from a passing vessel. The water here is some 30 feet deep. To a mariner unacquainted with the locality, or when a "norther" is blowing, this entrance is one of difficulty and danger.

Northeast of the city is the well-constructed castle of San Cristóbal, facing the ocean. It defends the city on the land side, occupying the whole width of the islet from the bay to the outer sea, pointing its fire in all directions. Its structure is accommodated to the nature of the ground, which is uneven, sloping from the northern or outer sea part to the bay. On the highest part of the hill is the ramp, through which the castle is entered. It has two large bombproof barracks and everything necessary in the way of office and storeroom. Upon these barracks is erected the Caballero Fort, with 22 cannon, whose fire dominates the city and its vicinity, on land and sea. Below the castle is the drill ground, with batteries directed toward the sea, the land, and the drawbridge of the interior fosse. Then follow three large ravelins, viz, San Carlos, occupying the top of the hill; Príncipe, situated on the slope of the Cuesta, and Principal, on which is situated the drawbridge of the second fosse, giving issue to the counter trenches, to the covered way, and to the field, which is reached through the gate of Santiago. All of these fortifications are in great part cut out of solid rock, and from the sea they offer to the view three tiers of batteries, one above the other, their fire being thrown in all directions.

This castle is connected with Morro Castle on the north by a wall of modern construction, there having been nothing on that side until the end of the past century but a few batteries, owing to the knowledge that the roughness of the coast rendered unnecessary any greater fortification to prevent a landing.

Starting from the southern part of San Cristóbal Castle and following the edge of the bay, a line of bulwarks is encountered, being those of Santiago and San Pedro, the curtain being interrupted by the España gate, after which follow the bulwark of San Justo and the gate of the same name, which forms an arch under the curtain; then follow the half bulwark of San Justo, the bulwark of La Palma or San José, the platform of Concepción, to the half bulwark and fortress of Santa Catalina, to-day (1887) the residence of the captain-general. From the fortress to the half bulwark of San Agustin to the west is found the gate of San Juan and then the platform of Santa Elena.

The construction of these fortifications was begun in 1630 and they were finished about 1641, but not until 1771 were the San Cristóbal Castle and the outworks built. These latter consist of a redan resting on the highest part of the glacis of San Cristóbal and called Fort Abanico (fan), on account of having this form. Between the town and the San Antonio Bridge are three small advanced lines. One consists of a running ditch and the other two of loop-holed batteries. At the head of the bridge is situated the San Antonio Fort.

On the extreme east of the islet and near the bridge above mentioned there is a small fort called San Jerónimo, which defends the passage over the bridge.

Between Morro Castle and the north coast near Palo Seco, there is in the middle of the entrance to the bay a small fort called Cañuelo; it is oblong, well fortified, and by its position obliges vessels, attempting to force an entrance to the port, to pass little out of rifle range between its fire and that of Morro Castle. Formerly, and in case of war, a chain was thrown out between this and Morro Castle to close the entrance to the port.

After rounding the bluff one finds a broad and beautiful bay, landlocked and with a good depth of water, which is being increased by dredging. It is by far the best harbor in Puerto Rico, and probably as good a one as can be found in the West Indies. However, it has its drawbacks. Sailing vessels are frequently detained by the northerly winds during the winter months, and even steamers with a draft of over 20 feet are sometimes delayed; but these occasions are rare. When they do occur, the "boca" or entrance to the harbor is a mass of seething, foaming water, and presents an imposing spectacle. To see steamers of 16 to 18 feet draft enter into a severe "norther" is a sight to be remembered, as the great waves lift them up and seem about to hurl them forward to destruction. At such times there is need of a stanch vessel, steady nerves, and a captain well acquainted with the channel, as no pilot will venture out.

The island upon which the city stands is shaped much like an arm and hand; it is about 2¼ miles long and averages less than one-fourth of a mile in width. The greatest width is a little over half a mile in the portion representing the hand, which also contains the major part of the city.

The mountains of Bayomon, which lie to the southwest of San Juan, are distant about 8 to 10 kilometers in a straight line from the city, and can be surmounted from the south. To reach them it is necessary to disembark to the west of San Juan, on the north coast of the island, between the towns of Dorado and Palo Seco. These mountains command the city.

San Juan is a perfect specimen of a walled town, with portcullis, moat, gates, and battlements. The wall surrounding this town is defended by several batteries. Facing the harbor are those of San Fernando, Santa Catalina, and Santa Toribio. Looking toward the land side is Fort Abanico, and toward the ocean the batteries of San Antonio, San José, and Santa Teresa, and Fort Princesa. The land part has two ditches, or cuts, which are easy to inundate. The fort and bridge of San Antonio, that of San Geronimo, and the Escambron battery, situated on a tongue of land which enters the sea. Built over two hundred and fifty years ago, the city is still in good condition and repair. The walls are picturesque, and represent a stupendous work and cost in themselves. Inside the walls the city is laid off in regular squares, six parallel streets running in the direction of the length of the island and seven at right angles.

The peninsula on which San Juan is situated is connected with the mainland by three bridges. The oldest, that of San Antonio, carries the highway across the shallow San Antonio Channel. It is a stone-arched bridge about 350 yards long including the approaches. By the side of this bridge is one for the railroad and one for the tramway which follows the main military highway to Rio Piedras.

Among the buildings the following are notable: The palace of the captain-general, the palace of the intendencia, the town hall, military hospital, jail, Ballaja barracks, theater, custom-house, cathedral, Episcopal palace, and seminary. There is no university or provincial institute of second-grade instruction, and only one college, which is under the direction of Jesuit priests. The houses are closely and compactly built of brick, usually of two stories, stuccoed on the outside and painted in a variety of colors. The upper floors are occupied by the more respectable people, while the ground floors, almost without exception, are given up to the negroes and the poorer class, who crowd one upon another in the most appalling manner.

The population within the walls is estimated at 20,000 and most of it lives on the ground floor. In one small room, with a flimsy partition, a whole family will reside. The ground floor of the whole town reeks with filth, and conditions are most unsanitary. In a tropical country, where disease readily prevails, the consequences of such herding may be easily inferred. There is no running water in the town. The entire population depend upon rain water, caught upon the flat roofs of the buildings and conducted to the cistern, which occupies the greater part of the inner courtyard that is an essential part of Spanish houses the world over, but that here, on account of the crowded conditions, is very small. There is no sewerage, except for surface water and sinks, while vaults are in every house and occupy whatever remaining space there may be in the patios not taken up by the cisterns. The risk of contaminating the water is very great, and in dry seasons the supply is entirely exhausted. Epidemics are frequent, and the town is alive with vermin, fleas, cockroaches, mosquitoes, and dogs.

The streets are wider than in the older part of Havana, and will admit two carriages abreast. The sidewalks are narrow, and in places will accommodate but one person. The pavements are of a composition manufactured in England from slag, pleasant and even, and durable when no heavy strain is brought to bear upon them, but easily broken, and unfit for heavy traffic. The streets are swept once a day by hand, and, strange to say, are kept very clean.

From its topographical situation the town should be healthy,

NOTES ON LOCALITIES. 37

but it is not. The soil under the city is clay mixed with lime, so hard as to be almost like rock. It is consequently impervious to water and furnishes a good natural drainage.

The trade wind blows strong and fresh, and through the harbor runs a stream of sea water at a speed of not less than three miles an hour. With these conditions no contagious diseases, if properly taken care of, could exist; without them the place would be a veritable plague spot.

Besides the town within the walls there are small portions just outside, called the Marina and Puerta de Tierra, containing two or three thousand inhabitants each. There are also two suburbs, one, San Turce, approached by the only road leading out of the city, and the other, Cataño, across the bay, reached by ferry. The Marina and the two suburbs are situated on sandy points or spits, and the latter are surrounded by mangrove swamps.

The entire population of the city and suburbs, according to the census of 1887, was 27,000. It is now (1896) estimated at 30,000. One-half of the population consists of negroes and mixed races.

There is but little manufacturing, and it is of small importance. The Standard Oil Company has a small refinery across the bay, in which crude petroleum brought from the United States is refined. Matches are made, some brooms, a little soap, and a cheap class of trunks. There are also ice, gas, and electric-light works.

The climate is warm and agreeable for nine months of the year, although one is subject, from the sudden changes, to cold and catarrh. The natives are particularly susceptible to this class of ailment, and to consumption and bronchitis.

The following authorities and corporations have their residence in the capital: A lieutenant-general, a field marshal, second in command in the province and governor of the garrison; a brigadier-general of the navy, chief of the maritime province, one of engineers, and another of artillery; a bishop of the diocesis, a subintendant, a subinspector of military sanitation, judge-advocate, war commissary, colonel, subinspector of the tercio of civil guard, and a comandancia of the same, as well as of artillery and engineers, a court, provincial deputation, treasury administration, etc.

Steamers frequently leave for Cuba observing the following itinerary: San Thómas (Jamaica), San Juan de Puerto Rico, Aguadilla, Mayagüez, Puerto Plata (Santo Domingo), Santiago de Cuba, Baracoa, Jibara, Nuevitas, and Havana. With rare exceptions the steamers running from Spain to Cuba stop at Puerto Rico. The government mail ships (Antonio Lopez Company) stop about ten hours, disembark mail and passengers, take on passengers, cargo, and mail for Havana, and continue on to Cuba. The mail ship which leaves Havana for Spain the 5th of each month, stops at San Juan de Puerto Rico, taking on board the mail and the passengers who are traveling on government business. Many foreign vessels also stop in the harbor. A submarine cable connects the island with Spain by the following route: From Puerto Rico to Kingston (Jamaica), thence via Cienfuegos or Batabanó to Havana, thence via Cayo Hueso to the United States, from whence it goes to England and finally to Spain.

Railroads: To Ponce via Arecibo, via Caguas and Cayey, via Humacao and Caguas. There is a post-office and telegraph station.

San Sebastian.—A town of 1,200 inhabitants, with a jurisdiction numbering 16,000; situated 14 miles from Aguadilla. It has a post-office and telegraph station.

Santa Isabel.—A municipal jurisdiction of 3,200 inhabitants, situated 63 miles from San Juan and 16 miles from Ponce. It has a post-office and telegraph station.

San Turce.—The fifth district from the capital, with 3,640 inhabitants. It is situated 3 miles from San Juan.

Toa Alta.—A town of 1,100 inhabitants, with a jurisdiction numbering 7,821; situated 15½ miles from San Juan. There is a second-class wagon road. The town has a post-office.

Toa Baja.—A municipal jurisdiction of 3,481 inhabitants, situated 10½ miles from San Juan. It has a post-office.

Trujillo Alto.—A town of 1,800 inhabitants, with a jurisdiction numbering 4,072; situated 15 miles from San Juan. The nearest railroad station is Rio Piedras, 7¼ miles distant. There is a post-office.

Utuado.—A town of 3,738 inhabitants, of whom 2,123 are white and 1,615 colored. It is the chief town of a jurisdiction of 30,045 inhabitants, 22,757 of whom are white and 5,306 colored. It is situated 56 miles from San Juan and 14 miles from Arecibo. There is a wagon road to the capital. There is a post-office and a telegraph station.

Vega Alta.—A town of 985 inhabitants, of whom 225 are white and 760 colored. It is the chief town of a jurisdiction of 5,420 inhabitants, 1,147 white and 4,275 colored. It is situated 22 miles from San Juan. The nearest railroad station is that of Vega Baja, 12½ miles distant. A first-class wagon road leads to this station. There is a post-office.

Villa de la Vega Baja.—A village of 2,531 inhabitants, chief town of the judicial district of its name. The municipal jurisdiction has 10,650 inhabitants. It is situated 23¼ miles from San Juan. There is a railroad station, a post-office, and a telegraph station.

Its church, which forms one of the facades fronting on the beautiful plaza, is in its proportions and general appearance one of the finest in the island. Its two towers are elegant, one containing a bell and the other the public clock. Opposite the church is the town hall, a fine building of rubble masonry of one story, but large enough to hold, besides the municipal offices, the jail and police station. The aspect of the square and of the whole village is very agreeable.

Yabucoa.—A town of 4,178 inhabitants, of whom 2,152 are white and 2,000 colored. It is the chief town of a jurisdiction of 12,862 inhabitants, of whom 5,655 are white and 7,207 are colored. It is situated 10 miles from Humacao, on the road from Humacao to Guayama. It has a post-office and a railroad station.

Yauco.—A municipal jurisdiction of 24,500 inhabitants, situated 15½ miles from San German. It has a post-office and a telegraph station.

It has a fine climate, good running water in abundance, is 50 meters above sea level, and has four commanding mountains. Here are also warehouses of stone and brick, capable of holding from 5,000 to 6,000 men. These are used to dry coffee, and are, or will be, vacant.

There is a large supply of pack mules and carts, which can be gotten at any moment for the handling of freight and supplies for the march to the capital.

NOTES ON LOCALITIES.

The following pages are extracted from the Annuario Militar de España for 1898, and give the strength and station of the Spanish troops in Puerto Rico on December 1, 1897. It is commonly supposed that very few changes have been made and that the figures, etc., are practically correct. For names of officers of the battalions in Puerto Rico, see the publication on Notes on the Spanish Army, June, 1898.

Résumé of the general, field, and other officers, those of assimilated rank, and enlisted men of the army of Puerto Rico.

Organizations.	Officers of the army.										Officers of auxiliary corps assimilated to—											Total.			Enlisted men.	Grand total.
	Captain-generals.	Lieutenant-generals.	Generals of division.	Generals of brigade.	Colonels.	Lieutenant-colonels.	Majors.	Captains.	First lieutenants.	Second lieutenants.	Generals of division.	Generals of brigade.	Colonels.	Lieutenant-colonels.	Majors.	Captains.	First lieutenants.	Second lieutenants.	Principal chaplains.	First chaplains.	Second chaplains.	Officers.	Assimilated.	Chaplains.		
General officers		1																				2				2
Corps of the general staff of the army					1	1	1	1														4				4
Infantry					1	3	11	17	52	96	35											214			5,000	5,214
Cavalry								2														2			8	10
Artillery					1	1	3	10	17													32			700	732
Engineers					1	1	1	5		3												11			200	211
Civil guard					1	1	2	8	12	10												34			746	780
Corps of military police (orden público)							1	2	5	1					1	1	1					9			187	196
Corps of military justice																		3					3			3
Administrative corps of the army																							8			8

SPANISH FORCES.

Military medical corps:																
Section of medicine							1	1	3	1	11				17	17
Section of pharmacy										2	2				2	2
Military veterinary corps										1	3				3	3
Corps of military equitation											1				1	1
Auxiliary corps of military offices									1	2	1				5	5
Sanitary brigade											1			21	1	22
Fortification guards											1				2	2
Ecclesiastical corps of the army												1	5		7	7
Total	1	1		7	14	27	78	131	49	3	2	7	7	18	1	5	1,357	42	76,862	7,219

Personnel of the permanent army of Puerto Rico.

The permanent army of Puerto Rico numbers during the present economic year (1897) 5,929 men, distributed in five battalions of infantry, one section of cavalry, one battalion of fortress artillery, one telegraph company, one section of workmen of the park, and a sanitary brigade. There is, besides, a tercio (regiment) of civil guard under the command of a colonel, composed of two commanderies, that of San Juan being under a lieutenant-colonel and that of Ponce under a major, and the corps of militia police (orden público), with a commandant, 8 officers, and 187 men.

Organizations.	Field and other officers.						Assimilated.												Enlisted men.	Animals.			Material.						
	Colonels.	Lieutenant-colonels.	Majors.	Captains.	First lieutenants.	Second lieutenants.	Surgeons.		Chaplains.			Veterinarians.			Professors of equitation.					Saddle.	Draft.	Pack.	Ammunition chests.	Guns.	Ammunition.	Section.	Catalan.	Forge.	Carriages.	Packs.
							First.	Second.	Principal.	First.	Second.	First.	Second.	Third.	First.	Second.	Third.													
One battalion of rifles (six companies)	...	1	2	8	19	7	1	1	...	1	...	...	...	...	...	...	...	1,000	3	1	...	...	...	...	...	1	...	...	...
One section of cavalry	...	...	...	...	...	...	...	...	...	...	...	...	...	...	...	...	...	8	8	...	...	...	...	...	...	...	...	...	...
One battalion of fortress artillery (five companies)*	...	1	2	7	17	7	...	1	1	1	...	...	1	...	...	1	...	694	7	1	38	...	51	...	...	1	...	...	...
Section of workmen of the park	...	...	...	...	...	...	...	...	...	...	...	...	...	...	...	...	...	6	...	...	...	...	...	...	...	...	...	...	...
Telegraph company	...	...	1	1	1	1	...	...	...	...	...	...	...	...	...	...	...	200	6	...	...	...	...	...	...	...	...	...	...
One sanitary brigade	...	...	1	1	1	3	...	...	...	...	...	...	...	...	...	...	...	21	...	...	...	...	...	...	...	...	...	...	...

Civil guard — commandery of San Juan		1	1	3	6	5	377	145
Civil guard — commandery of Ponce			1	4	6	5	360	105

* One of the companies is a mountain company.

There are besides in this district, as in that of Cuba, corps of volunteers, of whom only trumpeters and quartermasters are paid from the estimates. They are divided into 14 battalions, and 1 company in the Island of Vieques.

STATIONS AND STRENGTH OF SPANISH TROOPS IN PUERTO RICO.

TERRITORIAL DIVISION.

This captain-generalcy is divided into one military government and eight military commanderies, which are as follows:

Military government and commands.	Judicial districts.
Military government of the town of San Juan....	Capital.
Military commands of the departments of—	
Bayamón...	Capital and Vega Baja.
Arecibo...	Arecibo. Utuado, and Aguadilla.
Aguadilla..	Aguadilla.
Mayagüez..	Mayagüez and San Germán.
Ponce...	Ponce, Coamo, and San Germán.
Guayama...	Guayama, Coamo, Cayey, and Humacao.
Humacao...	Humacao and Guayama.
Island of Vieques.................................	Humacao.

CENTRAL BUREAUS.

Captain-general.—Lieut. Gen. Sabas Marín y González.

Aids: Lieutenant of Infantry ———; Captain of Infantry José González de Gelabert; Captain of Infantry Alberto González de Gelabert; Alvaro González Martínez.

Second in command in the district.—General of Division Ricardo Ortega y Díez.

Aids: Lieutenant-colonel of Cavalry ———; Major of Cavalry Miguel Núñez de Prado.

GENERAL STAFF OF THE DISTRICT.

General staff corps.—In command: Col. Juan Camo y Soler. Second in command: Lieut. Col. Francisco Larrea Liso. Maj.

José de Elola y Gutiérrez; Capt. Antonio Maury Rodríguez; Captain ———

Auxiliary corps of military offices.—Third Recorder Venancio Moreno Carpintero; First Official Nicasio Contreras Ortiz; First Official Julián Moreno Molina; Second Official Benito Sánchez Muñoz; Third Official Sebastián Escalona y Mons.

Auxiliary (representative of the general military chest of the colonies).—Captain of infantry, Miguel de Lasheras Grasite.

Permanent judges of the captain-generalcy.—Major of Cavalry Joaquín Palomino Díaz; Major of Infantry Santiago Escudero Ategui; Captain of Infantry Cecilio Martínez Jorcada; Captain of Infantry José Buj Piquer.

PRINCIPAL COMMANDERY, SUBINSPECTION OF ARTILLERY.

Principal commandant, subinspector.—Col. José Sánchez de Castilla.
Secretary.—Capt. Enrique Barbaza Montero.

GENERAL COMMANDERY, SUBINSPECTION OF ENGINEERS.

Principal commandant, subinspector.—Col. José Laguna Saint-Just.
In charge of documents.—Lieutenant Colonel ———, Maj. Rafael Rávena Clavero, Capt. Joaquín Barco Pons, Capt. Francisco Cañizares Moyano, Capt. Joaquín Gisbert Antequera.

MILITARY SUBINTENDENCY.

Military subintendant.—Subintendant Francisco de la Vega y López.
Chief of the section of inspection.—Commissary (First Class) Pedro Recax y Español.
Commissary of reviews.—Commissary (Second Class) Marceliano Cancio y Abajo; Commissary (Second Class) Ramón Poveda Bahamonde; First Official Eduardo Pérez Fillol; Third Official Luis Hidalgo y Salas; Third Official Alberto Belenquer Pielman; Third Official Ramón Tomás Ferrer.

DIRECTION AND SUBINSPECTION OF MEDICAL SERVICE.

Director and subinspector.—Surgeon Subinspector (First Class) José Batlle y Prat.
Secretary.—Chief Surgeon Pedro Pinar Moya.

AUDITORIAT.

Auditor of division.—José Sánchez del Aguila y León.
Lieutenant Auditor (First Class).—Onofre Sastre Canet.
Lieutenant Auditor (Third Class).—José Cabezas Piquer.

MILITARY INSTRUCTION.

PREPARATORY ACADEMY.

Director.—Colonel of Artillery José Sánchez de Castilla.
Professor.—Captain of Artillery Ramón Acha Caamaño, Captain of Artillery Fernando Sárraga y Rengel.

TOWN OF SAN JUAN.

Military governor.—General (Second in Command) Ricardo Ortega y Diez.
Secretary of the military government.—Lieutenant-Colonel of Infantry Francisco Sánchez Apellaniz.
Sergeant-major.—Lieutenant-Colonel of Infantry Francisco Figueroa Valdés.
First aid.—Captain of Infantry Rafael Noriega García.
Second aid.—First Lieutenant of Infantry Juan Díaz Sevas.

DEPARTMENT OF ARTILLERY.

Colonel.—The colonel of the principal commandery of the subinspection.

PARK.

Director.—The director of the principal commandery of the subinspection.
Documents.—Major ———; Captain of Works Ramón Acha Caamaño.
Interventor.—Commissary (Second Class) Ramón Poveda Bahamonde.
In charge of property and paymaster.—Third Official of Military Administration Luis Hidalgo y Salas.

DEPARTMENT OF ENGINEERS.

Colonel.—The colonel of the principal commandery of the subinspection; Fortification Guard (Second Class) Francisco García Zaya; Fortification Guard (Third Class) Francisco Orduña Burgos.
Supervisor.—Commissary (Second Class) Ramón Poveda Bahamonde.
Paymaster.—Third Official of Military Administration Alberto Belenquer Pielman.

ADMINISTRATIVE SERVICES.

Transports.—Commissary (Second Class) Marceliano Cancio y Abajo; Third Official Luis Hidalgo y Salas.
Factory of utensils.—Commissary (Second Class) Marceliano Cancio y Abajo; First Official Eduardo Pérez Fillol.

SPANISH FORCES. 47

MILITARY HOSPITAL.

Director.—Surgeon Subinspector (Second Class) Carlos Moreno y Lorenzo.

Chiefs of clinic.—Chief Surgeon Emilio Jerez y Huertas, Chief Surgeon Indalecio Garrido y González, Chief Surgeon Pedro Pinar Moya, First Pharmacist Antonio Ramos Rodríguez, First Pharmacist Francisco Sánchez Lahorra, Second Chaplain José Molina Jorge.

Supervisor.—Commissary (Second Class) Marceliano Cancio y Abajo.

Administrator.—First Official of Military Administration Eduardo Pérez Fillol.

GARRISON OF THE TOWN AND CASTLES.

Provisional Battalion of Puerto Rico No. 3, general staff and 3 companies.
Provisional Battalion of Puerto Rico No. 4, general staff and 3 companies.
Twelfth Battalion of fortress artillery.
Telegraph company.
Section of cavalry (escort).
Third Sanitary Brigade.
Battalion of Volunteers No. 1.

FIRST DEPARTMENT—BAYAMÓN.

Battalion of Volunteers No. 2.
Battalion of Volunteers No. 3.

SECOND DEPARTMENT—ARECIBO.

Military commandant.—Lieutenant-Colonel of Infantry Agapito Picazo Subiza.

Garrison.—Provisional Battalion of Puerto Rico No. 4 (1 company); Battalion of Volunteers No. 4; Battalion of Volunteers No. 14.

THIRD DEPARTMENT—AGUADILLA.

Military commandant.—Lieutenant-Colonel of Infantry Francisco Puig Manuel de Villena.

Garrison.—Provisional Battalion of Puerto Rico No. 4 (2 companies); Battalion of Volunteers No. 5.

FOURTH DEPARTMENT—MAYAGÜEZ.

Military commandant.—Colonel of Infantry Julio Soto Villanueva.

Garrison.—Battalion of Alphonso XIII; battalion of volunteers No. 6; battalion of volunteers No. 7.

FIFTH DEPARTMENT—PONCE.

Military commandant.—Colonel of Infantry Leopoldo San Martín Gil.

Garrison.—Battalion of rifles of the mother country No. 25; battalion of volunteers No. 8; battalion of volunteers No. 9; battalion of volunteers No. 10.

SIXTH DEPARTMENT—GUAYAMA.

Military commandant.—Major of Infantry José Reyes Calvo.

Garrison.—Provisional battalion of Puerto Rico No. 6; battalion of volunteers No. 11; battalion of volunteers No. 12.

SEVENTH DEPARTMENT—HUMACAO.

Military commandant.—Lieutenant-Colonel of Infantry Rafael Ubeda Delgado.

Garrison.—Provisional battalion of Puerto Rico No. 3 (2 companies); battalion of volunteers No. 13.

ISLAND OF VIEQUES.

Military commandant.—Lieutenant-Colonel of Infantry Luis García Alpuente.

Garrison.—Provisional battalion of Puerto Rico No. 3 (1 company); one company of volunteers.

SAILING DIRECTIONS. 49

The following pages are taken from "The Navigation of the Gulf of Mexico and Caribbean Sea," Vol. I, 4th edition.—The West India Islands, including the Bermuda Islands and the Bahama Banks.—Hydrographic Office Publication No. 86, Washington, 1898:

MONA PASSAGE AND THE ISLAND OF PUERTO RICO.

Mona Passage.—The channel between the islands of Haiti and Puerto Rico is clear of obstructions or dangers and is called the Mona Passage, from the small island of that name lying midway between Cape Rojo and Saona Island.

Mona Island.—Its summit is nearly flat, with a few bushes and trees, and it may be seen from a distance of 18 miles. It is of volcanic formation; its north, east, and NW. sides, consisting of high perpendicular bluffs, afford no landing place. On the west and SE. sides are a number of caves forming entrances to extensive subterraneous galleries which run in every direction. The surface of the island is composed of calcareous slate-colored rock, full of holes containing soil in which the trees and brushwood grow.

There are numbers of wild goats and hogs on the island, and turtles during the season.

A ridge of rocks run off the SW. point, and a vessel should not come inside the depth of 8 fathoms of water, which will be found at the distance of ¼ mile.

The eastern and northern parts of the island are said to be clear of danger and steep-to. The NW. end terminates in a promontory, and its extremity rises to a lofty perpendicular rock, which when on a bearing N. 6° E. (N. 6° E. mag.), or S. 6° W. (S. 6° W. mag.), has the appearance of a sail, with Monito open westward of it. From this end, named Cape Barrionuevo, round by south to the east end, the island is bordered by a bank of white sand and rocks with 18 to 3½ fathoms water on it. It extends off 1½ miles between Capes Barrionuevo and Julia, also called Caigo ó no Caigo Point (I fall, or I don't fall). It takes the latter name from an enormous rock on its summit which is very curiously balanced and threatens every moment to fall. Between Cape Julia and the east end of the island the bank extends off ½ mile.

Santa Isabella Bay is called by the fishermen Uvero Bay. The bottom is of sand, but there are so many rocks that vessels are apt to lose their anchors. Vessels can stand in without risk to a depth of 6 to 8 fathoms and then anchor. The holding ground, however, is bad, and a sea always sets in, so that a vessel must be ready to put to sea as soon as there is any sign of a hurricane from the west or when the south or SE. winds set in.

El Sardinero is the safer anchorage. It is only worthy of the name during the season of southerly winds. The sea in it is then smooth, as it is sheltered by Arenas Point and the spit which makes out to the westward from the latter. The bottom through-

1676——4

out the anchorage is white sand, without specks, and the depth from 8 to 12 fathoms. Still it must be remembered that outside of the shoal and on the parallel of Cape Barrionuevo the bottom is rocky and the water is very deep; hence it is necessary to stand well into the bight, where the bottom is white, without being alarmed at the rocky barrier at its head.

Landing.—In both Santa Isabella and Sardinero anchorages the beaches are so foul that a landing can only be effected with great risk. In Santa Isabella Bay, however, there are several boat channels through the reef or rocky heads, and in the center of the bay, SE. of the western point, there is a clear beach about 150 yards in length, where a landing may be effected under favorable circumstances by veering the boat in from a grapnel. The points forming this bay are shallow. These landings are well known to the fishermen, and with their assistance a boat may land, unless the sea is very heavy. During the season of the Northers both of the above anchorages are untenable, as the wind from the gulf and the current from the passage cause a tremendous sea.

Water.—A little to the right of the landing in Santa Isabella Bay there is a pathway leading to water under the southern cliffs, and here firewood will be found. Indifferent drinking water will also be found in the lower parts of the grottoes.

Tides.—The flood sets N. by E. and the ebb S. by W. at the rate of $\frac{1}{2}$ mile an hour. It is high water, full and change, at the island at 6h. 15m. and the rise is about 2 feet.

Monito lies about $2\frac{1}{4}$ miles N. 22° W. (N. 22° W. mag.) of Mona, with a clear channel between them. This little islet is somewhat circular, about 400 yards in diameter, and its sides are composed of steep, inaccessible cliffs, but much lower than those of Mona. It is quite barren, but frequented by numerous flocks of sea birds. At a distance its summit has the appearance of a shoemaker's last. There are 20 and 25 fathoms water at 100 yards from the west side of the islet. The only place where landing can be effected under favorable circumstances, but with much risk to the boat, is at a rock on the west side of the islet. Here, in a small angle or indentation of the shore, vessels have anchored for guano in a depth of from 30 to 36 fathoms.

Desecheo or Zacheo, the other island in this passage, lies N. 52° E. (N. 52° E. mag.), about 27 miles from the NE. point of Mona. The island is about a mile in circumference, and almost entirely composed of a remarkably lofty wooded hill, which may be seen at a distance of 36 miles. The few dangers which lie close to the shore always show themselves, and are steep-to. When seen from the SW. the south side appears very precipitous; but from the northward it appears more lengthened out, and it will be found a very useful object in navigating the western side of Puerto Rico. There is no anchorage under it.

Currents.—Near the sides of the Mona Passage there is generally a very perceptible current, frequently running to the north and NW. with a velocity of one or $1\frac{1}{2}$ miles an hour. In the middle of the passage the general direction of the current is with the wind to the SW. The tides, also, in some parts of the passage, run with great force, especially to the southward of Cape Engaño, where, during the month of May, a velocity of 3½ miles an hour has been experienced. The flood runs 9 hours to the SW. and the ebb to the NE. during 3 hours. Sometimes precisely the contrary duration occurs, and the tides have been known to run 6 hours in each direction. These irregularities necessitate great caution in navigating, and have doubtless been the cause of very many disasters.

Directions.—Mona Passage is much frequented by vessels bound from ports in the United States to the Spanish Main and neighboring islands, and by those from Europe bound to Jamaica and ports on the southern coasts of Haiti and Cuba. Especially is this the case in the winter, when the wind is apt to blow from the northward of east.

It has already been stated that there is no danger to fear this passage; but great caution must be used in the vicinity of Saona Island, which is low and foul, and a berth of at least 6 miles should be given it. Squalls are of frequent occurrence, especially in summer. They blow sometimes with hurricane force for a short time, and, although they often rise rapidly, always give warning of their approach.

Puerto Rico.—The island in 1509 was invaded by Spaniards from Haiti, and has since that time been a Spanish colony.

A range of lofty mountains called Luquillo, covered with wood and intersected by numerous deep ravines, runs through the center of the island, beginning near the NE. point and terminating south of Arecibo in a hill called the Silla de Caballo. The highest peak of this chain (3,714 feet high) is visible in clear weather from a distance of 68 miles. It forms an excellent landmark. It is called El Yunque, or Anvil Peak. In the interior are extensive savannahs, on which large herds of cattle are pastured, and along the coasts are tracts of level, fertile land.

The principal ports of export are San Juan and Arecibo on the north coast, Aguadilla and Mayagüez on the west, Guanica, Guayanilla, Ponce, and Arrayo on the south, and Humacao and Naguabo on the east coast.

The coasts of the island are by no means well known, and urgently need to be resurveyed.

On the eastern coast of Puerto Rico there are nine small rivers emptying into the sea, and several ports frequented by small vessels to load with sugar and molasses. The instructions which can be given for this coast are so deficient that it would be by no means safe for a stranger to cruise here without a pilot, who may be obtained at San Juan, St. Thomas, or sometimes at Port Mula, on Crab Island.

The population in 1880 was 666,000.

Hurricanes.—Although the island is south of the usual track of hurricanes, it has been severely visited by them. The cyclones of 1782 and 1825 were especially destructive.

Custom regulations.—A decree was issued in 1877 making it compulsory that all goods be consigned to an established merchant, so that merchants only can clear a package through the custom-house, and not then unless it is consigned to them. The rules concerning manifests are very stringent, and are in accord with those of Cuba. Fines from $25 to $1,000 may be inflicted for breach of custom regulations, and entire confiscation of ship and cargo.

Coal, when carried as sale cargo, is exempt from tonnage or discharge duties; other articles on board, however small, will subject the whole cargo to duties.

A bill of health certified by Spanish consul will be required. Vessels failing to present a manifest in the required form will be fined $500.

Port charges.—Interpreter, $4. Stamped paper, $8.75. Tonnage dues, $1 per ton of cargo, gross. Clearance, $1 to $8, according to value of cargo outwards. Sanitary visit: Vessels of 200 tons, $10; 250 tons, $11; 300 tons, $12; 350 tons, $13; 400 tons, $14; above 450 tons, $16. Labor costs $1 per day. Ballast, 50 cents per ton discharging. $1 per day for guard while marking.

Light.—On Cape San Juan a fixed white light, with red flash every three minutes, is shown at an elevation of 266 feet, and should be visible 18 miles. The lighthouse is cylindrical and dark gray in color.

Cordilleras.—A chain of islets and reefs, called the Cordilleras, extends from Cape San Juan for 11 miles. The eastern group of these islets is called the Barriles. They are steep-to, and between them and the Washer and Cactus cays there is a channel 2 miles wide and 10 fathoms deep.

Barriles Passage.—With a SE. wind a vessel bound northward may easily pass to the eastward of Puerto Rico and through this channel. It is also available for vessels bound from the north to any of the ports on the east or south coasts with NE. winds.

Hermanos Passage is formed between the Barriles and the Hermanos Rocks, and carries about 10 fathoms water.

San Juan Channel, between the head of the same name and the western extremity of the Cordilleras, is about ¾ mile in breadth and 9 or 10 fathoms deep. This is, in general, the best channel for vessels from the east coast of Puerto Rico with the wind from the NE. The western extremity of the Cordilleras, which forms the north boundary of the channel, is composed of two groups of rocks a little elevated. The easternmost of the two is named Icacos and the western group Cucaracha. The latter is nearly on the meridian of Cape San Juan.

Port Fajardo lies south of Cape San Juan. It is between Cueva Point on the north and Barrancas Point on the south, and has a depth of from 16 to 23 feet.

On a point abreast of Obispo Islet is a battery, and a few houses are scattered along the beach. The town of Fajardo is 1½ miles inland. Population, about 3,000.

The United States is represented by a consular agent.

This port is only a narrow canal, sheltered from easterly winds by three islets called Obispo, Zancudo, and Ramos, and also by a reef between the two latter having 6 to 12 feet of water on it, where the sea breaks in some places. The northern and southern ends of this reef form, with the islets of Zancudo and Ramos, two narrow cuts, having 23 feet of water. The southern passage is the widest, but neither should be attempted except in case of emergency.

There are two entrances into Fajardo. Through the southern one a depth of 18 feet may be carried, and it is entirely clear. It lies between Barrancas Point and Ramos Islet.

The northern entrance is between Cueva Point and Obispo Islet, and has from 4 to 6 fathoms of water. Nearly in the middle of the passage is a coral patch with only 6 feet of water on it, which requires great care to avoid. Although narrow, this channel is the best to enter by.

In approaching Fajardo from the eastward through the channel between Culebra and Crab islands, the navigator may choose from three channels: 1st, between the Cordilleras Reef and Palominos Island; 2d, between this island and the Largo Bank, and, 3d, between the Largo Bank and the chain of islets and reefs extending to the eastward, called Piraguas and the Lavanderas.

Although the first-named channel is the narrowest, it seems best, from the fact that all its dangers are apparent to the eye. With the wind from the NE. it leads to windward of the port. The depth in this channel is from 8 to 12 fathoms; in the second from 7 to 11 fathoms, and in the third from 6 to 8 fathoms.

Pilots cruise off the NE. point. To signal for them hoist national colors at foremast head. Pilotage (compulsory), $5 for vessel, without regard to size. For shifting berth, $2.

Quarantine dues.—If vessel is quarantined, $2 for each visit. Port warden's fees, $4.

Supplies.—Water, $1 per puncheon alongside. Vessel's stores, scarce and dear. Coal, $5 to $6 per ton alongside. Commissions on collecting freight, 2½ per cent; on disbursements, 2½ per cent; on procuring freight, 5 per cent.

Middle Channel.—To pass through this channel between Palominos and Largo Bank, the track lies about one mile south of Palominos Island.

The Southern Channel is bounded on the north by the Largo Bank, and on the south by the Piraguas and Lavanderas rocks and the Piñero Islands, with a width of 2 miles. In using it, keep Soldiers Point on Culebra Island, bearing S. 87° E. (S. 86° E. mag.) until the center of Palominos Island bears N. 17° E. (N. 18° E. mag.); the Largo Bank will have then been passed, and a course may be shaped towards Ramos Island to enter Port Fajardo by the southern passage.

Palominos is of moderate height, and covered with trees. Its shores are foul to the distance of ½ mile. Anchorage may be found about one mile off its western shore in 6 or 7 fathoms of water.

Largo Bank is narrow and steep-to. The sea generally breaks on it. As before stated, this bank forms the south side of the middle channel of approach to Port Fajardo.

Between Largo Bank and Ramos Islet there is a clear channel with 7 fathoms of water in it. The least water on the bank is said to be 13 feet.

Great and Little Piñero Islands are to the northward of Puerca Point, the eastern extreme of Puerto Rico. Farther to the eastward, and forming a chain of dangers, are the Lavanderas Rocks and the Piraguas. There are deep channels among these rocks and shoals, but without a pilot it would be prudent to pass to the eastward of them.

The Piñeros are two small islets, covered with wood and lying between Medio Mundo Point and Puerca Point, which is also low and wooded. On the western side of Great Piñero is a reef which extends northerly to Medio Mundo Point, forming a bar on which there is only 13 feet of water. The channel between this islet and the mainland is only fit for boats.

Between the reef which extends from the shore between these two points on one side and the reef skirting Great Piñero Island on the other there is a narrow bight where small vessels may anchor, but it is unsheltered to the SE. and south.

Little Piñero is nearly joined to the south end of Great Piñero by a reef, on which there are 13 feet of water. Near the eastern side of this islet there is a small detached rock, above water.

Descubridor is a small head between Little Piñero and the Chinchorros, lying about 1¼ miles southward of the western Lavandera. This danger is marked on the charts as of doubtful existence.

Lavanderas are two small rocks on which the sea generally breaks. They are steep-to, with 5 fathoms of water close to them, and about 1¼ miles apart.

Piraguas are two small, rocky islets, 1⅓ miles apart; they may be seen at a considerable distance, are steep-to, and have a clear passage between them, with not less than 5 fathoms of water.

Chinchorros are two dangerous shoals. The northern shoal is small and has 13 feet of water on it, with 5 fathoms all around. The southern shoal is ¾ mile long and ½ mile across, with only 5 feet of water on it; it is also steep-to. On both these shoals the sea generally breaks.

A vessel may pass between these dangers or between the northern shoal and the Piraguas. A more prudent course would be, however, south of all of them. Soldiers Point, kept on a bearing of N. 69° E. (N. 70° E. mag.) will lead clear of these dangers.

Caution.—Other shoals have been reported in this locality.

Bahia Honda.—This bay, a little westward of the south point of Puerca Island, is about a mile in extent, and open to the southward. It is protected by reefs which contract the channel from a mile to about ¼ mile in breadth. The eastern side of the bay terminates to the southward in a low, sharp point; the west side in a bold headland, crowned by a little hill. Near the latter a dry rock will be seen on the reef, and off the former the Cabras, two small, flat islets, covered with brushwood. The reef, which bars the entrance, skirts also the interior of the bay, and some of the patches within have only 13 feet of water on them, but these and the reef are easily seen. Aguas Claras River flows into the NE. corner of the bay.

Shoal.—A reef lies east, distant 2 miles from Cabras Island. There is a least depth of 12 feet of water on this reef, with from 13 to 26 feet all around; sandy bottom.

Directions.—To enter Bahia Honda, the south point of Puerca Island should be brought to bear about N. 12° W. (N. 11° W. mag.), when this course will lead up toward the entrance of the harbor. In entering, the eye from aloft will be the best guide for avoiding the reefs and shoal patches, and for picking out a clear spot for anchoring.

The anchorage has from 5 to 8 fathoms of water, but as it is open to the southward and is quite limited in extent, a large vessel had better lie outside in from 6 to 8 fathoms.

Algodon Bay.—From the western point of Bahia Honda to Lima Point the coast forms a large bay, in the middle of which is the islet of Algodon, moderately high, and near the coast. In this bay, which is sheltered from SW. round to NE., by way of north, the depth of water varies from 16 to 13 feet near the shore. Three small streams empty into it.

Just outside of a line drawn from Lima Point to Algodon Point are three shoals.

Algodon Bank, nearly ¼ mile in extent, with 2 fathoms water on it, lies with its eastern part on the meridian of the west part of Algodon Point, which is a large round headland, and from the southward presents a face nearly ½ mile in extent. The south part of the bank is about ½ mile from the point; the channel between is 400 yards in breadth, with 3½ to 4½ fathoms of water. In steering through, haul round Algodon Point, and anchor in 16 feet water.

Piedras Bank is separated from the Algodon Bank by a narrow channel. The position of this bank is doubtful, but it is supposed to lie with Algodon Islet, bearing between N. 52° W. (N. 51° W. mag.) and N. 71° W. (N. 70° W. mag.).

Lima Bank, a rocky ledge nearly awash, the sea generally breaking upon it, lies about ¾ mile S. 80° E. (S. 79° E. mag.) off Lima Point. It is about 600 yards in diameter. About 1¼ miles S. 43° E. (S. 42° E. mag.) of Algodon Islet there is said to be a sunken rock.

There is a good channel between the Lima and Piedras banks, in which the least depth of water is 10 feet, but as the position of the foregoing dangers can not be accurately given, the neighborhood must be approached with great caution.

The Port of Naguabo lies between Lima Point and Santiago Cay. At 1¼ miles west of Lima Point, Naguabo River empties. On its western bank is the little village of Ucaris, off which, in the mouth of the river, there is anchorage for a few coasters, with the wind from SW. round by north to east. Large quantities of cattle are exported from here to the other islands. The town of Naguabo lies 2 miles inland.

The United States is represented by a consular agent.

Dues.—Tonnage dues, $1 per ton; anchorage, $4; interpreter and doctor, $12; pilot and port captain, $16. These dues are for a vessel of 280 tons.

Santiago Cay is small and of moderate height. From its SE. side a reef extends in a SE. direction to the distance of one mile, and in some parts is nearly dry. Its northern shore is perfectly clear. Candeleros Point may be known by the little hill upon it, and between the point and the islet is Puerto Humacao.

Candeleros Point is bordered by a reef extending off a short distance. About one mile north of the mouth of Humacao River, which empties into the bay, are two small islets called the Morrillos.

No trustworthy directions can be given for the anchorage.

Humacao.—The town of Humacao is $2\frac{1}{2}$ miles inland, on the river of the same name.

Dues.—Pilot, in and out and entry, $36; interpreter and stamps, $12; anchorage and port captain, $26.50. These dues are for a vessel of 280 tons.

In approaching either Naguabo or Humacao, the best route is south of Crab Island.

Icacos Bay, south of Humacao, lies between Candeleros Point and Icacos Point.

Port Yabucoa.—Icacos Point is nearly 2 miles southward of that of Candeleros, and may be known by a small rocky islet near it. Port Yabucoa is between Guallane Point, which is a little southward of that of Icacos, and Yeguas Point farther on. Guallane River here runs into the sea. Yabucoa village stands about 2 miles in the interior, nearly abreast the west end of Crab Island.

Port Maunabo is formed by Cape Mala Pascua, the SE. end of Puerto Rico on the south, and Tuna Point on the north. The town is situated some miles in the interior, on the borders of the river which empties into the port.

Tuna Point Light is a flashing white light, showing a group of 2 flashes every 2 minutes, the flashes, each of about $7\frac{1}{2}$ seconds duration, being separated by an interval of 15 seconds, and followed by an interval of 90 seconds. It is 123 feet above the sea, and should be visible, in clear weather, from a distance of 18 miles.

The light-house, 53 feet high, consists of an octagonal tower, painted white, rising above a rectangular gray building.

General directions.—The sea on the east coast of Puerto Rico is generally smooth, so that vessels may lie comfortably in the anchorages. On leaving them, time will be saved by passing out through the Barriles or Hermanos Passage instead of running round the west end of Puerto Rico and out through the Mona Passage. Being off the SE. coast of Puerto Rico and near the entrance to the channel formed by it and Arenas Banks, when standing toward the Lima Bank, the west point of Bahia Houda should not be brought eastward of N. 27° E. (N. 28° E. mag.). When approaching the north end of the Arenas Reef, in standing to the southward do not open out Cape Mala Pascua off Narango Point. When El Yunque or Anvil Peak is shut in with the hill on the west point of Bahia Honda a vessel will be to the eastward of the Arenas Reef, and the southern boards may be prolonged.

Do not, however, bring Cape Mala Pascua to the westward of S. 64° W. (S. 65° W. mag.), which will avoid the Musquito, Corona, and Caballo Blanco banks, which lie off the north shore of Crab Island, in the neighborhood of Port Mula, and on which the sea does not always break. In standing to the northward, go no farther than to bring West Mountain, St. Thomas, in one with Soldiers Point, Culebra, N. 75° E. (N. 76° E. mag.), until to windward of the South Chinchorro Bank, which lies with the south point of Palominos in one with the westernmost Piraguas. When the latter is in one with Zancudo Islet, N. 51° W. (N. 50° W. mag.), a vessel will be to the eastward of the Chinchorros and eastward of the narrowest and most dangerous part of this channel, and may then work to windward.

When sufficiently far to the eastward, a vessel may pass out through the channel between the Barriles and Hermanos Islets or between Icacos, Cucarachas (the westernmost of the Cordillera), and San Juan Head, according as the wind may be to the northward or southward of east. The last being the westernmost, she may proceed through it as soon as she has rounded the eastern Piraguas, which, however, must be given a wide berth.

With the wind from the NE. a vessel may beat through in a day and a half, and from the SE. may run through in half a day.

With a pilot it may be accomplished in much less time, as follows:

Having cleared the north extreme of Arenas Bank, steer to the northward, so as to pass between the western Lavanderas and the Little Piñero, or between the Lavanderas, on which the sea always breaks. Steer east or west of the Largo Bank, and thence west of Palominos, and through the channel by San Juan Head; but to do this the wind should be to the southward of east. In passing between the Little Piñero and the western Lavanderas, bring the outer extremity of San Juan Head on a N. 18° W. (N. 17° W. mag.) bearing, which course will lead to the westward of Largo Bank and close up to the head. In taking this route the position assigned to the doubtful Descubridor Bank, said to be about south 1¼ miles from the western Lavandera and about the same distance from Little Piñero, should be carefully avoided.

These directions, however imperfect, will serve to point out the most prominent dangers and at the same time warn strangers not to get entangled among them without the assistance of a pilot.

The tides on the eastern coast of Puerto Rico run with great strength to the NE. 7 hours and to the SE. 5 hours.

The north coast of Puerto Rico is rugged and uneven; it runs in a nearly straight line east and west, and between San Juan Head and Port San Juan presents no shelter whatever. San Juan Head slopes gradually from the summit of the hills to the sea and terminates in a low, but clearly defined point; for about 14 miles westward from the head the coast is composed of dark, rugged looking cliffs, breaking down from the mountain side, but as the hills turn inward the land becomes low and undulating and appears to be well cultivated, many chimneys of steam sugar mills being seen above the trees. From off the west end of this high and cliffy portion of the coast, the fortifications and part of the city of San Juan will be seen. The shore appears to be skirted by a reef, inclosing numerous small cays and islets, over which the sea breaks violently, and it should not be approached within the distance of 4 miles.

A small rock, with 14 feet over it and 5 and 6 fathoms around, is said to exist about 20 miles eastward of Port San Juan and 3 miles offshore.

Los Embarcaderos Point will not be noticeable until well to the westward of it, when it will be seen projecting, low and covered with trees.

From Luquillo to the Loisa River the coast is low, with a range of hillocks 2 or 3 miles inland; back of Loisa is a hill, which, seen from the eastward, looks like an island. Between the Herrero and Loisa rivers and between Vacia Telegas and Maldonado points are white sandy beaches.

Vacia Telegas Point is formed by two low bluffs, covered with trees. Maldonado Point has the appearance from the eastward of an island.

Morro of San Juan will be easily recognized by the light-house. When within 5 miles of the entrance Cabras Island will open out; upon it are several buildings, and off the eastern end of it is the wreck of a steamer.

Port San Juan.—About 30 miles west of San Juan Head is the harbor and city of San Juan. The city is well laid out, and is one of the healthiest cities in the West Indies. It is situated on Morro Island, which forms the north side of the harbor, and is separated from the mainland by a narrow creek, called the channel of San Antonio.

The city is almost hidden from seaward by the high land on the northern shore.

The population is about 20,000. The sanitary condition of the city is good. The streets are clean and the people orderly.

The authorities to visit are the captain-general and the commodore of the station.

The United States is represented by a consul and vice-consul.

Coal can be had in any quantity. The amount usually on hand is about 3,000 tons, and costs $9 per ton. It is transferred to the ship by lighters, which hold about 10 tons each.

Provisions can be had; beef is quite poor; vegetables are good and quite cheap.

Water.—Either spring or rain water can be had at a cost of one cent per gallon. There are two water boats.

Quarantine is strict and well maintained. There is a quarantine station on an island. A health officer boards all vessels.

There are three hospitals—one military, which is for the use of the soldiers, and two private, which are small and cost $2 per day. For subscribers, only $1 per day.

Steamers of the Lopez line from Havana to Liverpool, three times a month; to Bremen, three times a month; Barcelona, four times a month; and the Atlas line.

Telegraph.—There is cable communication with St. Thomas; also a telegraph line connecting the principal places on the island.

Customs duties are high; nearly everything is taxed.

Pilots are efficient, but are not necessary for a steamer. Pilotage is $17 in and out and $4 for moving a ship in the harbor.

Lifeboat.—A lifeboat and life-saving apparatus have been established at San Juan.

Light.—The light-house on Morro Point exhibits a fixed light having a flash of five seconds' duration every minute. The light is elevated 171 feet above the sea, and should be visible 18 miles.

A semaphore is erected in the Morro fort, with which vessels may communicate by using the international code of signals. A black ball is hoisted on the gaff of the signal mast to indicate the probable approach of a storm.

San Juan Harbor.—Toward the east and south the harbor is sheltered by the low, swampy land of Puerto Rico, and on the west by the Cabras Islands and the shallow banks which connect them to the shore. The Cabras consist of four small islets and two small detached rocks close off their east end, the nearest of which lies 800 yards westward of the Morro Point; foul ground extends for nearly 400 yards off them. On Cabras Island (the largest) are two large hospital dwellings, and on the southernmost islet, called Canuelo, there is a fort which commands the entrance. Between the Morro and the Cabras the channel into the port is barred, and with strong northerly winds it breaks and becomes dangerous, although it carries a depth of from $4\frac{1}{2}$ to $5\frac{1}{4}$ fathoms.

Off Morro Island, at the eastern point of entrance, the ground is foul for about 200 yards, the eastern side of the channel being marked by a red buoy moored in 17 feet of water on the edge of the bank called St. Helena Shoal. The channel is here little more than 300 yards wide, its western edge being unmarked except by a wreck (of a steamer). Within this edge the western bank sweeps round, forming a deep bight, terminating in a sharp point at the Tablazo Shoal, on which is a red buoy, and farther in on the same side of the channel there is another red buoy.

St. Augustine Shoal also makes out from Morro Island to about 200 yards from the shore, nearly abreast of San Juan Gate. Its edge is marked by a red buoy.

Vessels of large draft, or those intending to make but a short stay, will find the most convenient anchorage between the St. Augustine and Tablazo shoals, abreast of San Juan Gate.

Puntilla Shoal extends about 300 yards southward of the sandy point of that name; the channel here is about 250 yards across, with 3½ to 6 fathoms water, its weather side being the deepest.

To the eastward of these sand spits is the inner port, with a depth of from 3½ to 4½ fathoms, and quite secure against all winds, but the water is very foul, owing to the number of sewers emptying into it. Punta Larga Shoal is marked by three red buoys; there is also one on the northern edge of Anegado Shoal. There are two mooring buoys for the English and French mail steamers, and in the inner harbor, eastward of the arsenal, is another mooring buoy for Spanish ships of war. Yufri Shoal has been dredged to a least depth of 25 feet.

The inner channel has, it is stated by various authorities, filled up considerably of late years, and there is probably less water there than is marked on the charts.

Directions.—Vessels entering this port are recommended to take a pilot, as dependence can not always be placed on the buoys marking the shoals being in position; and as vessels are seldom boarded by a pilot till within the harbor entrance, caution should be specially observed regarding the buoy intended to mark the SW. extreme of St. Helena Shoal, east side of entrance to the port. This buoy has at times drifted, and vessels run into danger.

Approaching from the eastward, run down the north side of the island at the distance of not less than 3 miles, until Salinas Point comes a little open to the northward of Great Cabras Island; keep on this line until the mouth of the harbor comes open, when steer for it, giving the Morro Point a berth of 225 yards, and having rounded the buoy on St. Helena Shoal, haul up for the anchorage abreast San Juan Gate; with the wind well to the northward this may be gained, but should it be southerly, having passed the Morro, shoot as far in as possible and anchor, towing or warping up when the wind falls. With the wind strong from the northward the sea on the bar frequently breaks and becomes dangerous. On account of the difficulty of steerage great caution must be used. In a sailing vessel, a pilot will be necessary for the inner port, where the holding ground is excellent, and the land eastward of the town being low, the benefit of the cool trade wind is felt, but, as before stated, the water is foul. No good leading mark can be given for the narrow channel between the outer anchorage and the Puntilla Shoal, and as the water is muddy, it can not be distinguished by the eye.

Inner harbor.—The channel to the inner harbor is marked by three red buoys on the port hand and two small light-red buoys on the starboard hand. From the outer harbor the passage to the inner harbor will look puzzling to a stranger, as more than this number of buoys will be visible.

To enter the inner harbor steer to pass the red buoy off San Juan Gate at 100 yards distance, and then between the red barrel buoy off the Barrio de la Puntilla and the two conical light-red buoys on Tablazo Shoal, keeping well over to the port hand. When abreast the inner conical buoy the barrel buoy off the end of Puntilla Shoal will not fail to be recognized, and it must be passed close to on the port hand, and two small red buoys on Punta Largo Shoal, off the city, brought immediately on the starboard bow, to avoid going on that shoal. Moor with open hawse to the NW. in the outer and to the NE. in the inner harbor.

Tides.—It is high water, full and change, in Port St. Juan at 8h. 2m.; springs rise about 1½ feet.

Coast.—The north coast of Puerto Rico from San Juan to Arecibo, a distance of 33 miles, affords only indifferent anchorages, of which Manati is the best.

Manati River.—Coasters and other vessels which ship the produce of this coast anchor either at the mouth of the river, where there is no shelter and where landing is impracticable in bad weather, or at Palmas Altas, which is more secure with ordinary winds. In fair weather the coast may be approached within a mile, in depths varying from 15 to 26 fathoms.

Tortuguero is a small town on the shore, about 20 miles westward of Port San Juan. This part of the coast as far as Arecibo should not be approached within 3 miles.

Arecibo River, having its outlet east of the town of that name, has 3 feet of water on its bar. When much flooded the river forms another channel to the westward; but this entrance is always dangerous on account of the reefs which skirt that part of the coast. The river rises in the mountain chain which traverses the island in an east and west direction; and between Utuado, a town near its source, and Arecibo, a considerable trade in provisions is carried on by means of rafts.

Between Arecibo and Aguadilla the coast affords no shelter even for coasting vessels.

Arecibo is a small reef harbor of considerable commercial importance, about 12 miles westward of Tortuguero, but in the winter season it is only safe for small vessels that can get inside the reef. At that period vessels of large draft will find anchorage on the bank, about 2 miles off shore, but they will ride heavily and must be prepared to slip the moment the wind threatens to veer to the northward or westward. In the months of April, May, June, and July vessels of moderate draft may venture farther in and anchor under the reef in from about 3½ to 4 fathoms water.

The town stands on the western side of the bay, and is protected by a circular fort to the eastward of it. About a mile to windward of the town a tower and signal post will be seen on a steep hill. Near the center of the reef is the cut or channel for small vessels, and at the east end, between it and the cliff, there is a passage for boats.

There is a rivulet of excellent water, deep enough to admit launches, at the NE. end of the bay, near the town of Arecibo.

The United States is represented by a consular agent.

Port charges.—For a vessel of 226 tons, with ballast in and cargo out, the expenses were $408.

Light.—A fixed white light is intended on the Morillo de Arecibo (Punta Morillo), east side of Arecibo road.

The light is 120 feet above the sea, and in clear weather will be visible about 18 miles.

The light-house is a rectangular building with a hexagonal tower attached, both painted white.

Coast.—From Arecibo to Agujerada Point, 24 miles to the westward of it, the northern coast of the island is flat, low, and sandy. It there takes a SW. direction for a mile, and is formed of bold, rocky cliffs. Bruquen Point may be rounded within a mile, where the depth will be from 20 to 25 fathoms; but the coast here is fringed with reef and must be cautiously approached.

Light.—From a red masonry light-house on Bruquen Point is exhibited, at an elevation of 65 feet, a light visible 14 miles. The light is flashing red and white alternately every ½ minute, and is reported irregular.

West coast.—From Bruquen Point the coast curves outward to the SW. for about a mile and then becomes low and sandy as far as Peñas Blancas Point, which is covered with trees.

Aguadilla Bay.—On the northern shore of this bay is the town of San Carlos de Aguadilla, on the banks of the river from which it takes its name.

Toward the southern part of the bay is the village of San Francisco.

The town of San Carlos is an excellent place to obtain water and all kinds of provisions.

Vessels of any size may anchor here with ordinary wind, but during the winter months a heavy swell rolls into the bay. The only dangers are the reef off Peñas Blancas and the sand bars at the mouths of the small streams, which extend off about 400 yards.

A narrow bank of soundings, about ¼ mile wide and very steep-to, skirts the shore. In anchoring, be careful not to do so too near the edge of the bank, as a vessel is liable to drag off. In the winter time it would be prudent to be prepared to go to sea at once upon any indication of a shift of wind to the north or NW.

A good berth will be found with the church in the town of San Carlos bearing S. 84° E. (S. 84° E. mag.) and the north point of the bay N. 11° W. (N. 11° W. mag.), in 18 fathoms, about ½ mile from the shore. In approaching Aguadilla Bay from the southward, care must be taken to keep Jiguero Point to the eastward of N. 11° E. (N. 11° E. mag.) to avoid the foul ground which extends as far to the southward as the SW. point of the island.

The population of the district is about 12,500. The Atlas line of steamers calls here.

Rincon Bay is between Jiguero Point on the north and Cadena Point on the south. The bottom is foul and affords no good anchorage.

Jiguero Point Light is a fixed white light. The light, 69 feet above the sea, should be visible, in clear weather, from a distance of 8 miles.

The light-house, 38 feet high, is a rectangular building with an octagonal tower rising from the center.

Pelegrino Reef has 10 feet of water over it, and on it four vessels have been lost. It lies about one mile off the coast, midway between Cadena and Jiguero Points. The reef is not discernible in ordinary weather, and caution is necessary when navigating in this vicinity.

Cadena Point, 4 miles southward of Aguadilla Bay, should not be approached within the distance of a mile.

Añasco Bay lies between Cadena and Algarrobo Points. There are many factories in the neighborhood. The Añasco River empties into the bay, and has thrown up a shallow bar before it, which extends more than ¼ mile from the shore. Outside this there is well-sheltered anchorage, with the prevailing winds for vessels of the largest draft. The outer Las Manchas, the northern of the outlying shoals off this bay, with only 2 fathoms water on it, must be carefully avoided.

Mayagüez Bay lies between Algarrobo and Guanajibo Points, and is about 3 miles wide and 1½ miles deep. In the northern part of the bay the depth gradually decreases from 10 to 4 fathoms towards the shore, but shoals extend across the entrance, requiring great attention in working in. The anchorage affords excellent shelter from northerly winds, and admits vessels of large size, and is undoubtedly the best anchorage in the island.

From Algarrobo Point (which may be known by a house with a red roof, built upon high piles on the hill just above the point) the coast of the bay trends to the SE. for 1¼ miles to Little Algarrobo, a low, sandy point, on which there is a sugar factory, with a chimney and some blue buildings around it. There are two sugar factories with high chimneys situated at the northern part of this bay, about ¼ mile north of Algarrobo Point. The shore between is foul for 600 yards off; and ½ mile SW. from Algarrobo Point lies the reef of that name, which at the outer part is nearly dry and steep-to.

At about ¼ mile southward of Little Algarrobo Point, at the head of the bay, is the entrance to the Mayaguez River, in which small droghers lay up for the hurricane season. The river is a ditch of the smallest proportions, almost dry at the entrance. There is an iron bridge across it, and before it is the best anchorage, sheltered from the northward round by east to SW., with good holding ground. Thence the low shore bends round to the SW., with shallow water some distance off, and north 1½ miles from Guanajibo Point a spit runs off nearly a mile from the shore.

Mayagüez is a thriving town, healthy, lighted with gas, and has excellent water. Tram cars run from the custom-house to the town.

The town is clean, orderly, and well kept. Generally but one family lives in a house. Yellow fever is sometimes epidemic. The temperature in summer ranges from 75° to 90°.

There is telegraphic communication with the principal ports of the island.

The authority to visit is the military commandant.

The United States is represented by a commercial agent.

Supplies.—Provisions are expensive.

Water can be had, both spring and rain water. Cost, $2.50 per ship, no matter what quantity is taken. Ship's boats must be used.

Quarantine is not very strict. There is a health officer. There are two hospitals—one private, which has six beds for foreign seamen at a cost of 50 cents per day; also a military hospital, for the use of the soldiers.

Port charges.—Pilot and harbor-master's fees, $10. Interpreter, $4. Tonnage dues, $1 per ton of cargo. Health visit: Vessels of 150 tons, $9; and on each 50 tons in excess of 150, $1 additional. Custom-house fees, in and out, and stamped paper, $17.50. Discharging ballast: Sand, 50 cents per ton; stone, free; ballast guard, $2 per day. Discharging general cargo, $10 per load of 40 tons.

Lights.—Two small red harbor lights shown from the wharf serve as a guide to boats at night for the landing place.

Buoys.—All the buoys at the entrance to the harbor are painted white.

The tide rises and falls in Mayagüez Bay from 2 to 3 feet, but no exact determination of the time of high and low water has been made. The periods are said to be irregular.

Guadeloupe Reef.—In 1876 the French mail steamer *Guadeloupe* ran aground while entering Mayagüez Bay. The following bearings were taken while the vessel was aground: Jiguero Point, N. 20° W. (N. 20° W. mag.); Desecheo Island, N. 60° W. (N. 60° W. mag.). No information has been received as to the vessel's draft or as to the depth of water on the bank.

Tourmaline Reef.—Westward of Mayagüez, an extensive reef having as little as 4 fathoms of water over it, and possibly less, was recently passed over by H. M. S. *Tourmaline.* From the reef the peak of Cerro Montuoso (8 miles eastward of Mayaguez) bore east (east mag.); Desecheo Island, N. 30° W. (N. 30° W. mag.). The bottom is apparently of coral, with remarkable white stripes extending north and south across it. The bottom was visible in 12 fathoms.

Outer Las Manchas is the northern and outermost of the shoals at the entrance of Mayaguez Bay, and lies N. 68° W. (N. 68° W. mag.) about 2½ miles from Algarrobo Point. It is about ¼ mile in extent, with from about 2 to 4 fathoms water on it, and sometimes breaks. The dark, discolored water may be seen at a little distance.

Inner Las Manchas lies ¾ mile S. 45° E. (S. 45° E. mag.) of the Outer Las Manchas. It is ¼ mile in extent with 2 to 3 fathoms water on it. Between it and the Algarrobo Reef there is an inner channel a mile wide, with 5¼ fathoms in it.

Allart Bank.—This bank, on which a Danish frigate of the same name struck in 1833, is about ¾ mile in length and ¼ mile in breadth, with from 1½ to 2½ fathoms water on it; the shallowest part lies N. 17° W. (N. 17° W. mag.) of Guanajibo Point and S. 56° W. (S. 56° W. mag.) 2 miles from Algarrobo Point. The passage between it and the Inner Las Manchas is ½ mile in breadth, with from 3½ to 4½ fathoms water, and is the principal channel leading to the anchorage of Mayaguez.

Rodriguez Bank.—The northern edge of this shoal is about 1¼ miles to the southward of the Allart and just without the line of the bay. It is about ¼ mile in extent and dry in several places. Between the Rodriguez and the Allart there is a bar with 13 to 16 feet water over it.

The channel between Rodriguez Bank and Guanajibo Point has 13 feet least water and is used only by coasters.

Pierre Blanche (white rock) is a small patch of one fathom, lying just within the line of the Allart and Rodriguez banks, at about an equal distance from each. It obstructs the passage between these banks.

There is said to be good anchorage to the westward of the Mayagüez Banks, but in the absence of trustworthy information of the neighborhood it should be approached with caution.

Directions.—A good mark for entering Mayagüez Bay through the channel between Allart Bank and Inner Las Manchas is Cerro Montuoso Peak in line with the northern and higher hummock of a wooded, saddle-shaped hill bearing S. 79° E. (S. 79° E. mag.).

For a steamer, or for a sailing vessel with a fair wind, the best course will be found by bringing Montuoso Peak over the custom-house, bearing S. 73° E. (S. 73° E. mag.).

The custom-house is near the water's edge, and is the most southerly of four large houses with flat roofs, lying close together. The church on with Montuoso Peak also leads over the bar of the Mayaguez River, in 12 feet of water. If the buoys are in place a vessel has only to steer in midway between them.

In beating in, a vessel may stand toward Las Manchas (inner) until the custom-house and church are one; but to the southward, toward the Allart Shoal, she must tack before the peak of Montuoso comes in line with the church, until within the two shoals. When the land to the southward of Guanajibo Point is shut in with that point bearing south a vessel will be eastward of the outer banks. In coming from the northward, the channel may be taken between Las Manchas and the Algarrobo Reef. In this case take care not to haul in around Algarrobo Point until the peak of Montuoso opens south of the chimney of Vigo's sugar house, which is white and a conspicuous object near the shore north of the Puntilla Battery.

With a large vessel it is advisable to take a pilot.

Coast.—The coast between Mayagüez Bay and Cape Rojo is foul and bordered by rocky shoals which extend fully 1½ miles seaward. The approaches to this part of the coast are rendered dangerous from the want of definite knowledge as to the positions of the various offlying rocks and shoals.

Port Real de Cabo Rojo, about 9 miles south of Mayaguez Bay, is almost a circular basin ¾ mile in diameter, with a depth of 16 feet in the center. The channel, which is very narrow and tortuous, carries 9 feet water, and lies near the south part of the entrance. From the north point an extensive reef runs off, which, after skirting Cay Fanduco, terminates at Varas Point. The inhabitants in this locality subsist chiefly on fish; boats leave here during the season for the turtle fisheries of Mona Island.

Boqueron Bay.—About 2 miles from Port Real is Guaniquilla Point, and between it and that of Melones, 2½ miles farther on, is Boqueron Bay. It is obstructed by numerous shoals both within and without. It may be entered by two channels, having not less than 4 fathoms water, which lead into a spacious and sheltered anchorage.

Boqueron Bay appears to be the line of separation as regards the climate and productions of Puerto Rico. On the north side, where there is an abundant rainfall, the country is fertile, covered with trees and rich pasture lands, where cattle feed. To the south, toward Melones Point, and having its rise there, is a chain of arid mountains without trees or pasture; an uninterrupted drought does not permit the growth of vegetation on this side, but it will be seen from the following description that the shoals off this end of Puerto Rico, between Mayaguez and Cape Rojo, are so numerous and so imperfectly known as to render it not only difficult but dangerous to approach either of the above places.

Negro Shoal is of small extent, and almost always breaks. It lies 3¼ miles from the nearest part of the shore, with Guanajibo Point bearing N. 85° E. (N. 85° E. mag.), and Jiguero Point N. 8° W. (N. 8° W. mag.).

Media Luna Shoal is said to be a reef ⅔ mile long and about 400 yards wide. The sea sometimes breaks upon it. From its north end Guanajibo Point is said to bear N. 62° E. (N. 62° E. mag.) and Jiguero Point N. 6° E. (N. 6° E. mag.); ½ mile east of it are said to be three rocks on which the sea breaks constantly, but the existence of both shoal and rocks is very doubtful.

Las Coronas are sand banks about ½ mile in extent, which just cover, and sometimes break. They lie to the southward of Negro Shoal, with Guanajibo Point bearing N. 37° E. (N. 37° E. mag.), and Jiguero Point N. 3° W. (N. 3° W. mag.) 3¼ miles from the coast.

Guaniquilla Shoal is not marked on the Spanish chart, but is said to lie 2 miles westward of Guaniquilla Point. It is a rocky ledge, 400 yards in extent, with 16 feet of water on it.

Gallardo Bank is also a rocky ledge, which lies nearly 6½ miles west of Melones Point. It is 600 yards in extent, and has 16 feet of water on it. Halfway between this bank and the shore another 16-foot shoal is shown on the charts.

Mount Atalaya is the highest and northernmost of two peaks at the western extreme of the chain of mountains which runs from east to west in the NW. part of the island. It has a noticeable appearance and forms an excellent landmark.

Cape Rojo, the SW. point of Puerto Rico, is a bold bluff sloping down from a hill with two peaks. Seen from the east or west it has the appearance of two small islands close to highland. When seen from the southward two remarkable bluffs are seen to the eastward of it.

A good fishing bank of clear white sand and coral, called the White Grounds, extends 8 or 9 miles from the cape, on which the depths are from 6 to 15 fathoms; the edge is very steep-to, and the bottom is visible in 12 or 13 fathoms.

Light.—A light-house is erected on Cape Rojo, from which, at an elevation of 128 feet above the sea, a white light revolving every minute is exhibited, visible 18 miles; the building is hexagonal in shape. The light has been reported irregular.

The south coast of Puerto Rico is generally foul, and should be very guardedly approached, for there is very little correct information respecting it. It appears, however, that in some parts soundings extend to a considerable distance from the shore, and the lead should, therefore, be well attended. In running down, it is advisable not to come within 4 or 5 miles of the land. From the offing, this side of the island appears lofty, but the shore is generally low and bounded by mangroves. Sixteen small rivers empty into the sea from this shore, but few are capable of admitting even boats. There are many small harbors and anchorages under the reefs, known to the fishermen and droghers, and one or two capable of receiving vessels of a large draft. The south coast of Puerto Rico, Lieut. Zuloaga remarks, is incorrectly shown on the existing charts, and should not be approached within a distance of 6 or 7 miles without great caution.

From Corcho Point, one mile SW. of Cape Mala Pascua, the coast curves to the northward and westward, then to the southward, forming a bay into which the Guardawaya River empties. Viento Point forms the western limits of this bay and the eastern limit of the bay of Patillas, the western limit of the latter bay being Figuera Point. No accurate information can be given with regard to these bays, but they are believed to be more or less obstructed by reefs.

Light.—A light is exhibited from a light-house on Figuras (Figuera) Point. The light is a fixed white light, visible through an arc of about 180°, or from Cape Mala Pascua eastward, to Obras Grande Point westward. It is 47 feet above the sea, and should be seen, in clear weather, from a distance of 12 miles.

The light-house, 44 feet high, consists of an octagonal tower, painted a light gray color, rising above a rectangular building of black, white, and light gray colors.

Port Patillas, in Patillas Bay, is situated about 3 miles inland on the left bank of the Chiquito River.

Guayama Reef.—Its outside edge is at an average distance of 3½ miles from the shore. It is divided into three parts, the eastern being named Media Luna, the middle Algarrobo, and the western Ola Grande.

Vessels sailing along this part of the coast are cautioned to keep well outside of this reef.

Arroyo is a small bay immediately westward of Figuera Point. It can be easily recognized by the village of Arroyo, lying 3 or 4 miles inland and visible 12 or 15 miles. There is a white church on a little hill above the village, having on its western end a square tower and a cupola on the eastern end.

The United States is represented by a consular agent.

Anchorage.—The anchorage may also be recognized by the custom-house, a large yellow building. The center of the town bearing about north leads in through the passage between the reefs, which is stated to be about one mile in width. This bank is a spit running off from the eastern reef, and will be cleared by keeping the middle of the village of Arroyo bearing N. 22° E. (N. 23° E. mag.).

A good berth is ¾ mile offshore, with the custom-house bearing north (N. 1° E. mag.). This anchorage is not all well sheltered, and a constant SE. swell is felt, and vessels anchor with port anchor with a spring in the cable, or run a kedge to keep head to the swell.

Port charges.—Vessels calling in ballast pay captain of the port pilotage, $10; health visit, according to tonnage, $10 to $15; interpreter, $4; stamped paper, if the vessel takes cargo, $10; custom-house fees, $4; tonnage dues, $1 per ton.

Guayama, although merely an open roadstead, is secure with the ordinary winds and much frequented. The anchorage possesses excellent holding ground, and is protected to the eastward against the trade winds by a reef, 3 miles in length, which extends between 3 and 4 miles from the shore. It lies about 12 miles westward of Cape Mala Pascua, and may be recognized from an offing outside the reef by a guardhouse on the shore, which bears about N. 10° E. (N. 11° E. mag.) of the west end of the reef, and a windmill on a hill a mile to the westward of it. To the eastward of the reef, between it and the cape, the depth is from 10 to 7 fathoms at 2 or 3 miles from the shore, and 13 fathoms at a mile outside to the southward of it. As the anchorage is approached the soundings become very irregular, varying from 5 to 8 fathoms until within the reef, when they gradually decrease as the shore is neared; the lead must therefore be well attended.

Directions.—When approaching Guayama roadstead from the eastward—or indeed if bound to either of the ports on this side of the island from that quarter—Cape Mala Pascua should be given a berth of 4 miles, and when it bears to the eastward of N. 1° W. (north mag.) the Guayama Reef will generally come in sight from aloft. Shape the course to pass well outside, paying attention to the lead, and when the guardhouse bears N. 10° E.

(N. 11° E. mag.) haul in toward it, under the west end of the reef, and steer boldly in. The church kept open a little eastward of a prominent hill in the interior is a good course in. The best anchorage will be found in 4 fathoms water, about a mile from the shore, with the guardhouse on the same bearing, and the west end of the reef S. 12° E. (S. 11° E. mag.). In leaving the bay, if bound westerly, steer out S. 22° W. (S. 23° W. mag.), but a good offing must be obtained before bearing up, in order to avoid the cays and reefs to the westward. The whole coast line of the bay is wrongly chartered and the shoals are farther from shore than shown.

Vessels when passing along the south coast of Puerto Rico and in the vicinity of Arroyo Bay should exercise great caution, in order to avoid the dangers fringing the shore.

Port Jobos or Boca del Infierno.—About one mile to the westward of Port Guayama a narrow peninsula runs to the westward for 3 miles, which, with a couple of islands lying off its western end, forms Port Jobos or Boca del Infierno. No trustworthy information is attainable with regard to this port. Several small streams from the hills inland lose themselves in the swamp at the head of the bay, none of them emptying directly into the sea. The port is formed between Poznelo Point on the east and Colchones Point on the west.

Port Aguirre is at the head of the bay between Colchones and Arenas Points.

Port Salinas de Coamo is well sheltered by reefs. The entrance may be easily distinguished by several cays lying near Arenas Point and a guardhouse about 4 miles to the northward of the western cay. The channel lies between this western cay and a reef 1¼ miles west of it, on which the sea always breaks.

Coming from the eastward, after bringing Cape Mala Pascua to bear north, distant 4 miles, the course will be S. 84° W. (S. 84° W. mag.), which will carry a vessel outside all the cays lying along shore.

Steer boldly in between the outer or westernmost of the cays lying off Arenas Point and the reef 1¼ miles to the westward, passing the cay at a distance of 200 yards. Stand in toward the guardhouse and anchor with it bearing N. 6° E. (N. 6° E. mag.) about one mile distant, in 4 or 5 fathoms of water.

Discolored water extends for some distance to the southward of the cays. Three miles off shore the depth is 10 fathoms, decreasing to 7 fathoms as the coast is approached.

In leaving this harbor a vessel should, if bound to the westward, stand to the southward until Muertos Island bears to the northward of west (west mag.) before keeping away.

Nina Shoal.—Within the harbor is a rocky shoal, with 16½ feet on it, with 22 feet all around.

Water.—There is a good watering place in Port Salinas de Coamo on the shore near a lagoon, about ½ mile to the westward of the guardhouse.

Coamo Bay.—Its shore is skirted by reefs throughout its length. The Coamo River empties into the bay. Near Coamo Point are several small cays, and 2 miles to the southward are the Berberia Cays, with dangerous banks near them. Petrona Point is the eastern extremity of the bay.

Boca Chica.—The reef continues to the westward around Coamo Point as far as Port Pastillo. Boca Chica is a small trading place, and the approach to it is said to be clear of dangers. Soundings should be carefully attended to.

Port Jacagua is situated at the mouth of the small river of the same name, $1\frac{1}{2}$ miles west of Boca Chica. To the westward of the mouth of the river are two small cays, called the Frios. This port is said to be easy of access, but no exact directions can be given. As the soundings diminish regularly from $6\frac{1}{2}$ to $3\frac{1}{2}$ fathoms in approaching the shore here, the lead will be a good guide.

Muertos or Dead Chest Island lies 4 miles off the south coast of Puerto Rico and nearly midway between the SW. and SE. points of the island. The southern part of the island is high and rocky, sloping toward the north, and from a distance looks like a separate island. The island is nearly connected to the coast of Puerto Rico by a reef extending from its NE. point, on which the sea generally breaks heavily. This reef seems to skirt the east and south sides of the island. In the latter direction it extends $\frac{1}{2}$ mile off shore. At about 200 yards distance from the SW. end of the island there is a small flat rock, called the Hammock, with a dry reef between them. The Hammock should not be rounded nearer than $1\frac{1}{2}$ miles. Four hundred yards southwestward of the Hammock there is said to be a rock with 8 feet on it.

Water can be obtained on Dead Chest Island by digging wells a little above high-water mark. Turtles are plentiful in the proper season, and the neighboring banks abound with fish.

Anchorage.—The western side of Muertos Island is free of danger, and affords fair anchorage in from 7 to 12 fathoms water. A good berth may be taken with the NW. point of Muertos in one with the northern hill bearing east (east mag.), in 8 fathoms, sand, at about $\frac{1}{4}$ mile from the shore; or with the western extreme of Hammock Cay S. 20° E. (S. 20° E. mag.), distant $1\frac{1}{2}$ miles, and the north point of Muertos N. 50° E. (N. 50° E. mag.).

Light.—From a tower standing in the middle of a T-shaped building on the SW. point of Muertos Island a light is shown at an elevation of 297 feet and should be visible 18 miles. A flash of three seconds duration is shown every three minutes.

Berberia Cays.—Three miles N. 67° E. (N. 67° E. mag.) from Muertos Island are two cays named Berberia, and in their neighborhood are many dangerous banks, very imperfectly known. With the island bearing west, distant 3 or 4 miles, the depth is 6 fathoms. From the hills white water is seen a considerable distance to the eastward; the lead must, therefore, be well attended. The cays are joined by a reef. From the larger and northern cay a shoal of considerable size extends NW. and SW., on which there is only 6 feet water. These two cays are often submerged, and are dangerous to approach on the west and south sides; but to the northward of the larger there is good anchorage in 4½ to 7 fathoms, mud.

There is said to be a clear channel north of Berberia Cays with 5½ fathoms least water.

Great caution must be observed by the navigator in this vicinity.

The Bay of Ponce is nearly 3 miles across between Carenero, the eastern, and Cucharros, the western point; the port is in the NE. corner of the bay, and on its shore is the village of Port Ponce, containing 1,500 inhabitants. The custom-house, a long, white, two-storied building, with flat roof and flagstaff, is the most prominent object in the village, and is very conspicuous from seaward. The shores are low and bounded by mangrove and cocoanut trees, but 2 or 3 miles westward of Cucharros Point the land rises and becomes hilly. Ratones Island is low and covered with brushwood; its surrounding reef, which nearly dries at low water, stretches off southeastward for 600 yards. Arenas Cay is small and bushy.

Cardones Island is low, covered with brushwood, and in its center is a wooden house. A reef surrounds the island to the distance of about 400 yards.

Light.—There is a fixed red light on Cardones Island, elevated 46 feet above the sea, and it should be visible in clear weather from a distance of 10 miles.

The light-house, 39 feet high, consists of a cylindrical tower with a red cupola rising above a rectangular building, which is white in color, with blue panels.

Cayito Reef is a dangerous coral bank which seldom breaks. There are 9 feet on its eastern edge, and probably shoaler water will be found. A white chimney open eastward of the negro huts, near the cocoanut grove on the north side of the bay, bearing north (north mag.), clears the east side of the bank. There is a 7-fathom channel between Cardones Island and Cayito Reef, but it should not be taken without a pilot. The Gatas, four small, low cays off Carenero, appears as a continuation of that point; its projecting reef, upon which the sea breaks, is steep-to. At the extremity of the reef off Peñoncillo Point northward of Carenero are two small rocks which uncover 4 feet at low water. Cabrillon Point lies about ¾ mile eastward of Carenero Point; two small islets or cays lie off it.

Vessels approaching Port Ponce should not come within 5 miles of the land until the light-house bears N. 68° E. (N. 68° E. mag.), which should then be steered for, passing westward of Tasmanian Shoal. When abreast of Cardones Island, alter course to N. 11° E. (N. 11° E. mag.) for anchorage. The fore and main masts of a steamer wrecked on Tasmanian Shoal show two-thirds above the water.

The town of Ponce has a public hospital and is lighted with gas. It is connected with Jamaica by a telegraph cable, and also has telegraphic communication with the principal places on the island.

The law holds the masters of vessels responsible and liable to fines for any false declaration in contents, quantity, weight, or measure.

The United States is represented by a consular agent.

Supplies.—The supply of coal and wood is uncertain. Water is scarce and bad. Vessels' stores, being mostly imported, are high.

Port charges.—Tonnage dues, $1 on each ton of cargo; health dues on vessels of 100 tons, $8, and $1 for each 50 tons in excess up to 450; $16 for all over 450 tons; pilotage in and out, $10; tug-boat charged by agreement; wharfage, for each lighter load of cargo, $1; sand, per lighter, $5; interpreter and duplicate manifest, $12; stamp paper, entrance and clearance, $10; fort pass, $2; hospital fee, $4; taking in stone ballast, per ton, $1.50; sand ballast, per ton, $1; ballast guard, $1; horse hire for filling molasses casks, per puncheon, $6\frac{1}{4}$ cents; water delivered alongside, per puncheon, $1; labor, per day, $2; stevedore, per hogshead, 20 cents; coal, from $7 to $12 per ton. Cargo is handled by lighters. Vessels with clean bills of health are quarantined for twenty-four hours; vessels from infected ports, from eight to forty days.

Harbor rules.—No vessel is allowed to change her anchorage without permit from harbor master; fine for doing so equals double pilotage. All vessels from foreign ports are obliged to wait the sanitary and revenue visit. Vessels in quarantine will fly a quarantine flag. All boats must come alongside the wharf in front of the custom-house. No vessel can ballast or unballast without permission of the harbor master. Mineral coal is considered as ballast. No vessel can leave after sunset or before sunrise. Colored men as passengers or crew can not land.

Tasmanian Shoal (or Brillante), on which the *Tasmanian* grounded, has $3\frac{1}{2}$ to 5 fathoms of water over it; this shoal ground is nearly circular with a diameter of about 600 yards; as little as $13\frac{3}{4}$ feet have been reported on the east side of the shoal.

From the shoalest part, the center of Ratones Island is in line with a remarkable fall in the hills bearing N. 77° W. (N. 77° W. mag.), and a conspicuous clump of trees on the middle (the second) range of hills behind the town is in line with the east extreme of Ponce Village N. 11° E. (N. 11° E. mag.)

The conspicuous clump of trees in line with the house of the captain of the port (the house next west of the custom-house) bearing N. 14° E. (N. 14° E. mag.) leads westward of the shoal. The saddle hill, nearly on the same line of bearing, and given as a leading mark on the chart, is not easily distinguishable.

Eastward of Tasmanian Shoal, $\frac{1}{4}$ mile distant, is another patch of shoal ground; this is about 400 yards in diameter, with $3\frac{3}{4}$ to $4\frac{1}{2}$ fathoms water on it. There is a depth of $6\frac{1}{2}$ fathoms between the two shoals.

Buoy.—A bell buoy, surmounted by a ball and painted red, has been moored in 3 fathoms water, on the west edge of the Tasmanian Shoal.

Directions.—Shoal and uneven soundings exist southward of the bay for some distance from the shore, probably on irregular banks extending from Ratones Island on the westward and from Muertos Island on the eastward, leaving a deep channel between them into the port, eastward of Cardones Island. Approaching from the westward, the custom-house open of the east end of Cardones Island, bearing N. 28° E. (N. 28° E. mag.), crosses the bank in 5¼ fathoms, and on nearing Cardones, open the custom-house to N. 17° E. (N. 17° E. mag). From eastward, round Hammock Cay, at the distance of 1½ miles, and steer N. 59° W. (N. 59° W. mag.); on nearing the port the shipping and upper part of the custom-house will be seen over the low mangrove trees, and small vessels may cross in four fathoms water, with the custom-house in line with the west end of Gatas Islets. Large vessels should bring the custom-house to bear N. 17° E. (N. 17° E. mag.), on which bearing the least water will be 13 fathoms, and when abreast of Gatas steer north (north mag.) to the anchorage. The edge of the bank is 1¼ miles southward of Cardones Island. Pilots can always be obtained, but they only board vessels when off Cardones. The land breeze often sets out between sunset and sunrise.

Tides.—It is high water, full and change, in Ponce Harbor at 2h. 0m. (approximately) and the rise 2 feet, but they are very irregular.

Port Matansa is a small bay open to the southward. The Peñuelas River empties into it. Ratones Island serves as a mark to the entrance to this port. From Port Matansa the coast trends SW. to Guayanilla Point, between which and Majagua Point is the Bay of Guayanilla. Near Guayanilla Point are several small islands. Majagua Point is skirted by a reef.

Port Guayanilla is a large bay, almost circular, open to the southward. Several small rivers empty in the bay. There is anchorage in this port in 5¼ fathoms water; the entrance is open on a N. 11° W. (N. 11° W. mag.) bearing.

To the westward of the port the coast is foul.

The town of Guayanilla is situated on the banks of the river of the same name, about 1¼ miles from the entrance.

Port Guanica.—This port is an inlet about 1¼ miles in length in a NW. and SE. direction, and ¼ mile in breadth, with a depth of 3¼ fathoms water at its inner end and 4¼ fathoms at its eastern, over a sandy bottom. It is the best harbor on this side of the island, and lies about 15 miles eastward of Cape Rojo. The depths in this port are shoaling on account of the alluvium carried down by the rains. A mud bank, with a few scattered rocks extending from the north shore almost to the center of the port, has only 2 feet water.

Its entrance, formed between two bold headlands, Meseta Point on the east and Pescadores Point on the west, is little more than 200 yards wide, and is in the middle of a large bay formed between Brea Point, a bold and rocky cliff, and Picuda Point, 3 miles eastward of it.

Close off Picuda Point are two small islets, called Caña and Caña Gorda. Between them and Meseta Point an unbroken semicircular reef sweeps round outwards to the distance of ¾ mile from the shore, and without this, 800 yards off, there is a detached narrow, rocky ledge 600 yards long in a north and south direction, with a depth of only 12 feet water on it. The south end of this ledge lies S. 23° E. (S. 23° E. mag.), a mile from Meseta Point, and on the line between Brea and Picuda Points. The western shore, between Pescadores and Brea Points, recedes into a deep bight, which is blocked up by a reef extending across from the former to within ¼ mile of the latter, and is steep-to.

Light.—A light is exhibited on Meseta Point. The light is a fixed white light, 118 feet above the sea, and visible, in clear weather, from a distance of 8 miles.

The light-house, 40 feet high, is a rectangular building with an octagonal tower rising from its center.

Directions.—Approaching Port Guanica from the eastward, run down outside the reefs until Meseta Point is in line with the western pap of Caña Gorda, which may be easily recognized. This mark will lead in close alongside to the westward of the outer ledge in 10 fathoms water. The point on with the eastern pap will lead more in mid-channel, and when Caña Gorda bears N. 84° E. (N. 84° E. mag.) a vessel may steer for the center of the channel into the harbor. Run boldly through between the entrance points, and take up the most convenient berth within, where there is nothing in the way. The SW. shore is the boldest; but the farther a berth is chosen to the eastward, the easier it will be to sail out. In beating up from the westward, Brea Point may be passed at the distance of 200 yards, then steer for Point Meseta until the middle of the entrance bears north (north mag.) when stand in and anchor.

Coast.—From Brea Point a broad chain of reefs, known as the Margarita, extends as far as Cape Rojo; the south extreme of the reef extends fully 4 miles off shore and forms a point to leeward of the village of Parguera. This chain of reefs affords three passages, which are only accessible to vessels of light draft and which no vessel should attempt without the aid of a pilot.

Terremoto Passage.—In the neighborhood of Salinas Bay, between Carcovado Point and Terremoto Cay (the largest of the outer cays), is Terremoto Passage, where the soundings are 4½ to 7 fathoms, and by which coasting vessels enter Salinas Bay.

Faluch or Middle Passage is near Cabras or Mateo Island, and has 9¾ fathoms of water. The eastern edge is marked by a small mangrove cay, from which a reef extends to the NW. Faluch Passage, the best of the three, leads to the port of Guijano, which is formed by the coast and an inner line of reefs, and has a depth of 7 to 9 fathoms. The port is spacious, deep, and sheltered from all seas.

Indio Passage, the western one, is about 4 miles westward of the Middle Passage. It is abreast of Pitajaya. It is about 400 yards broad and has 7 fathoms of water inside. Anchorage, sheltered from the sea, is found under the lee of the reefs.

Cape Rojo and light. Page 351.

Winds.—The winds around Puerto Rico appear to be of the same character as those met with at the Virgin Islands. There is no regular land breeze to take advantage of, although the usual trade wind generally slackens during the night in the immediate vicinity of the shore. Under the west end the wind in the daytime will incline inward. In the winter months north and NW. winds sometimes occur, and blow hard; and in the summer long calms and light SE. airs prevail, with terrific squalls and heavy rains, especially on the south side. From the absence of any remarks on the rollers, we may conclude that they are at least not so heavy or so dangerous as at the Virgin Islands.

Currents.—On the north side of Puerto Rico the current is said to incline generally to the SW. or towards the shore, and to run with greater velocity in the winter than in the summer months. On the south side its course is generally west, but its movements are here uncertain. Some navigators state that at the full and change of the moon a strong weatherly set will occasionally be found, especially if light winds or northers have prevailed near these periods, and consequently gives great assistance to vessels beating to windward. In February it has been found running a knot an hour to the northward; in the summer months it will incline to the NW. towards the shore, and round the SW. end into the Mona Passage with great force.

www.ingramcontent.com/pod-product-compliance
Lightning Source LLC
Chambersburg PA
CBHW022128160426
43197CB00009B/1197